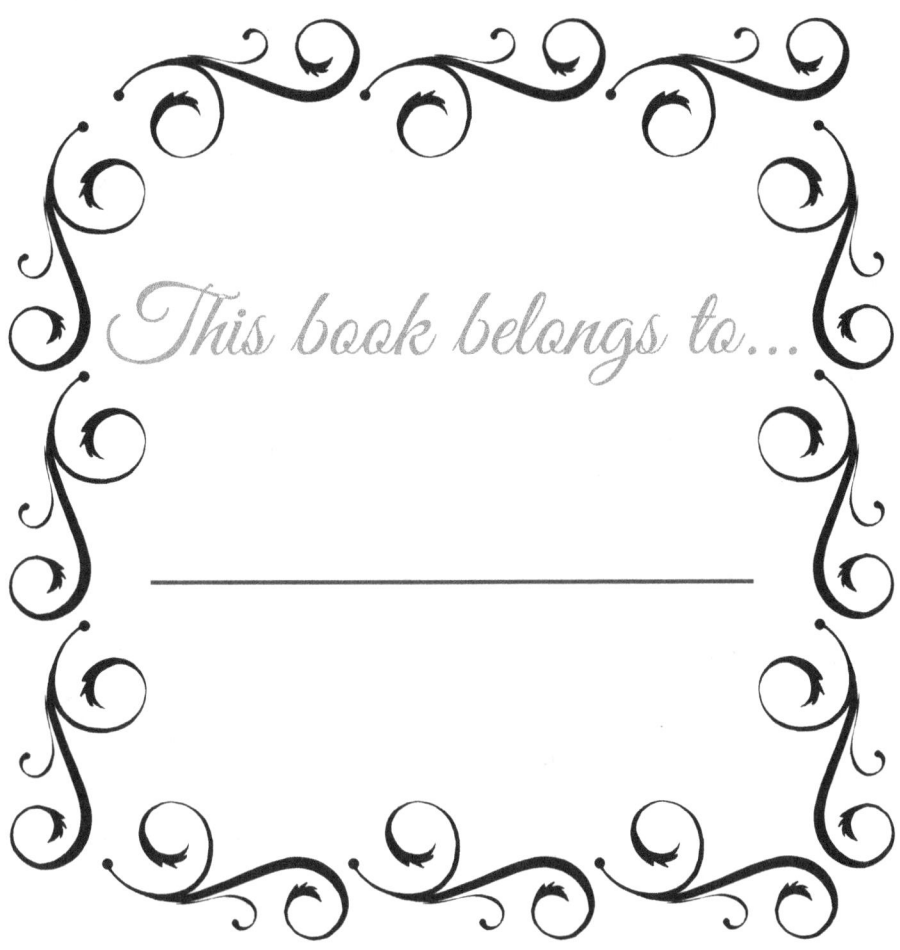

This book belongs to...

_____

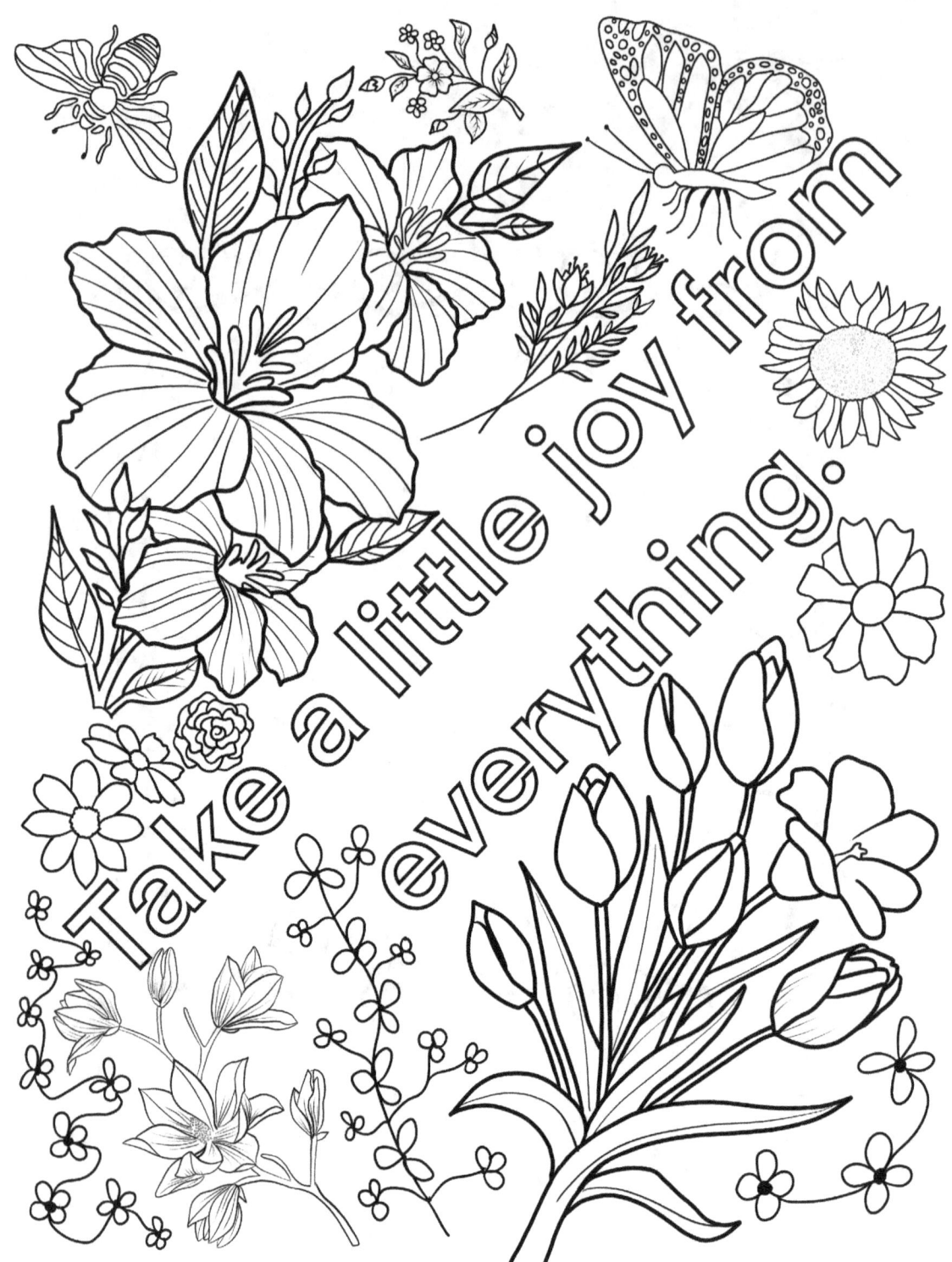

Copyright 2020 Ron Yarosh Books

No portion of this book may be reproduced or copied by any means including electronic or mechanical without the express permission of the author.

Violators will be prosecuted.

Dear colorist friend,

Thank you very much for purchasing my latest and fabulous Adult Coloring Book. I hope you enjoy adding your colorful creative touch to the images in this edition called, **Inspiration and Relaxation**.

I'm sure you will find it inspirational, a bit challenging…and perhaps somewhat stimulating.

As Horace said, "A picture is a poem without words."

More of my unique adult coloring books are in the process of being created and published. Look for them on Amazon and other publishing platforms

If you like this book, please give me a review, and tell your colorist friends about it.

Now, let the fun and inspiration begin. Get out your favorite colors and start to relax.

Your friend,

Art King

REMEMBER TO PLACE A SHEET OF PAPER BETWEEN YOUR COLORING PAGES TO AVOID THE POSSIBILITY OF BLEED THROUGH TO THE FOLLOWING PAGE.

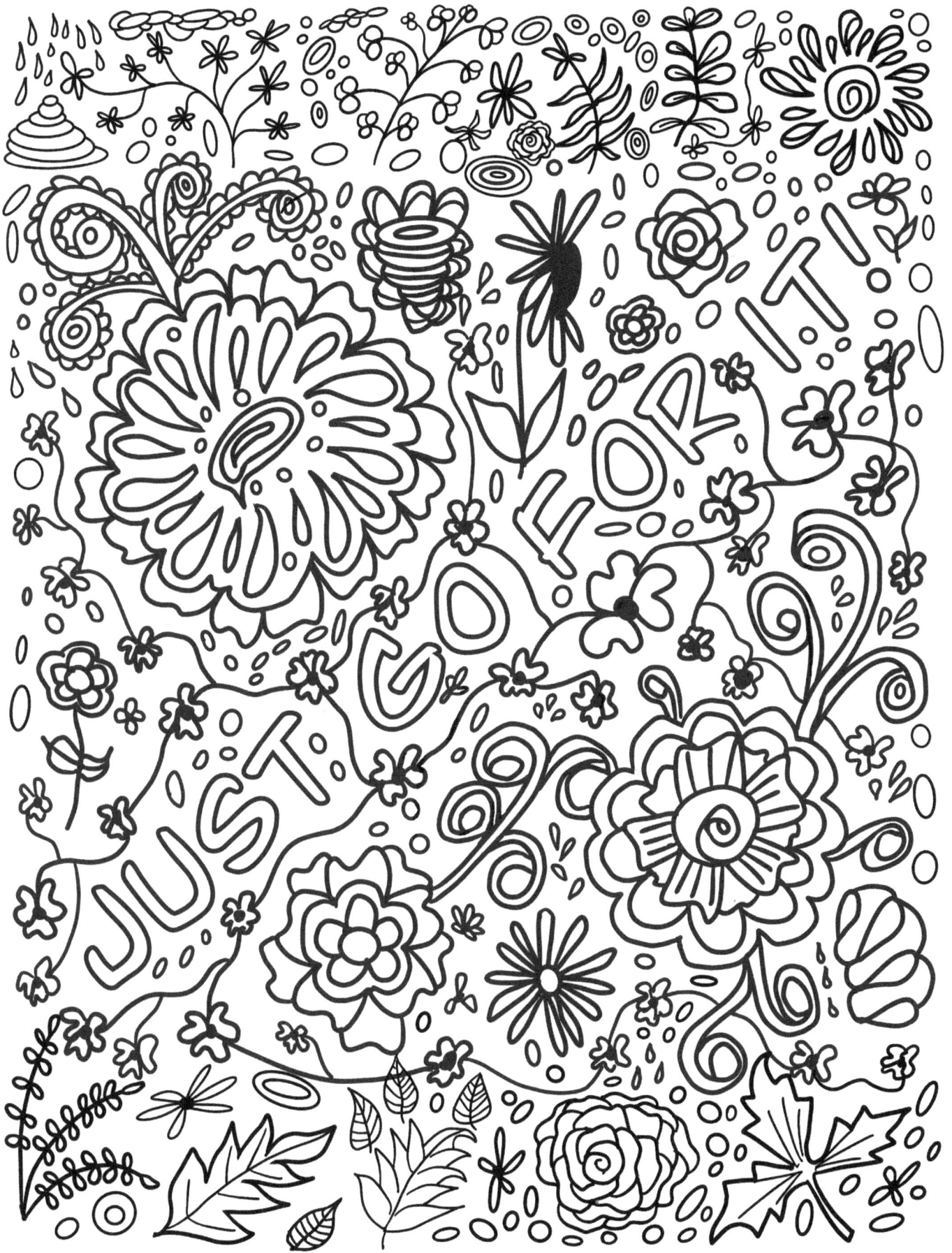

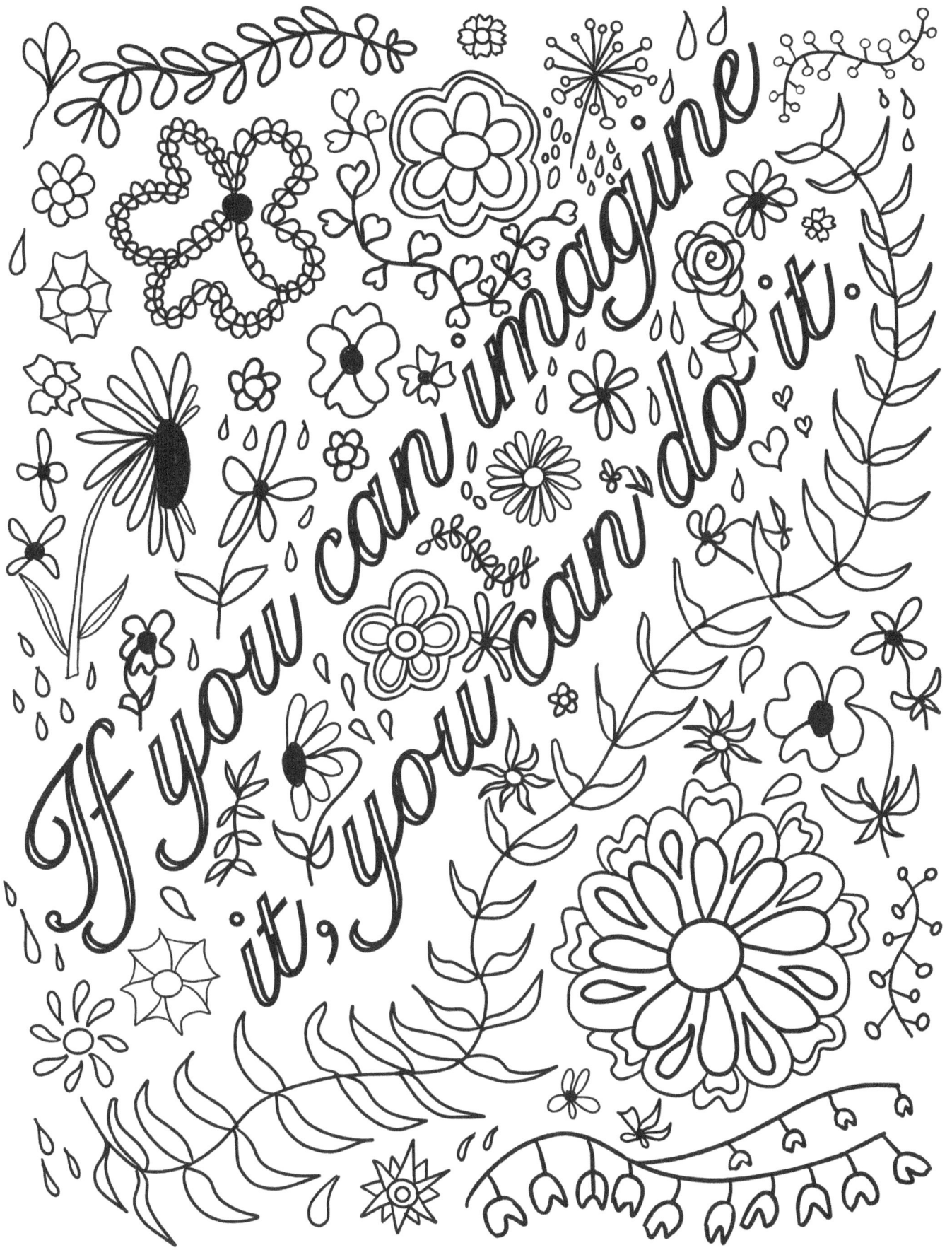

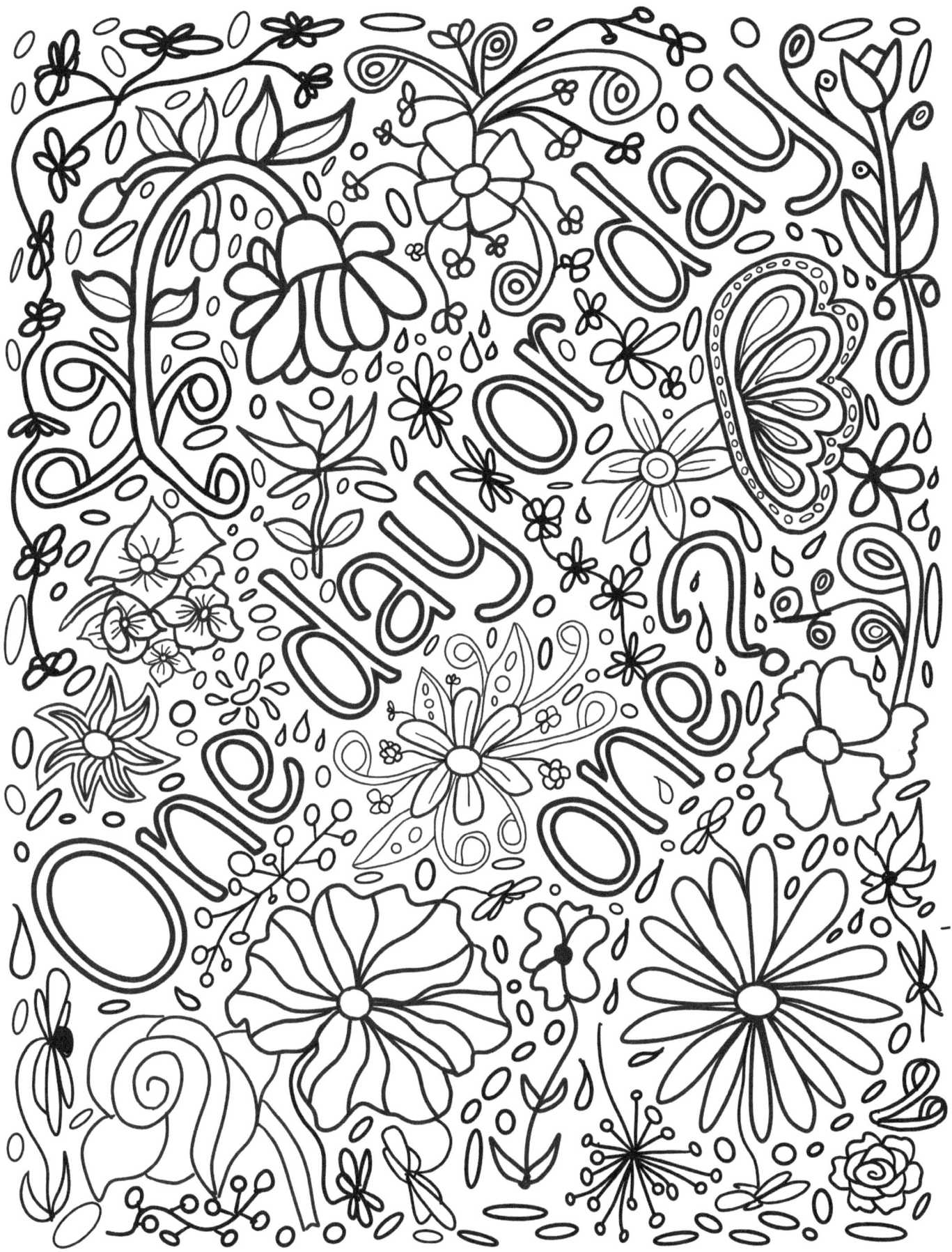

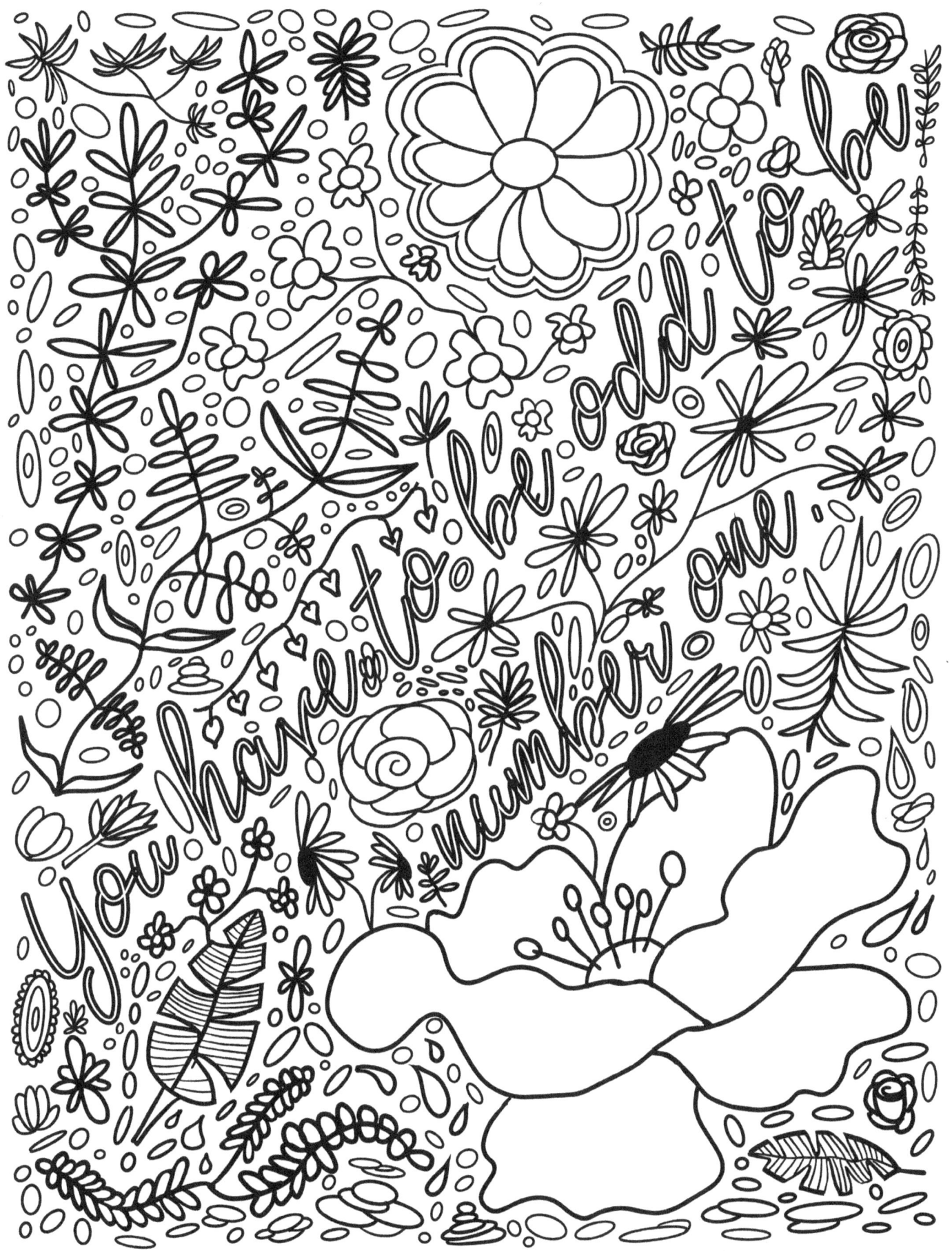

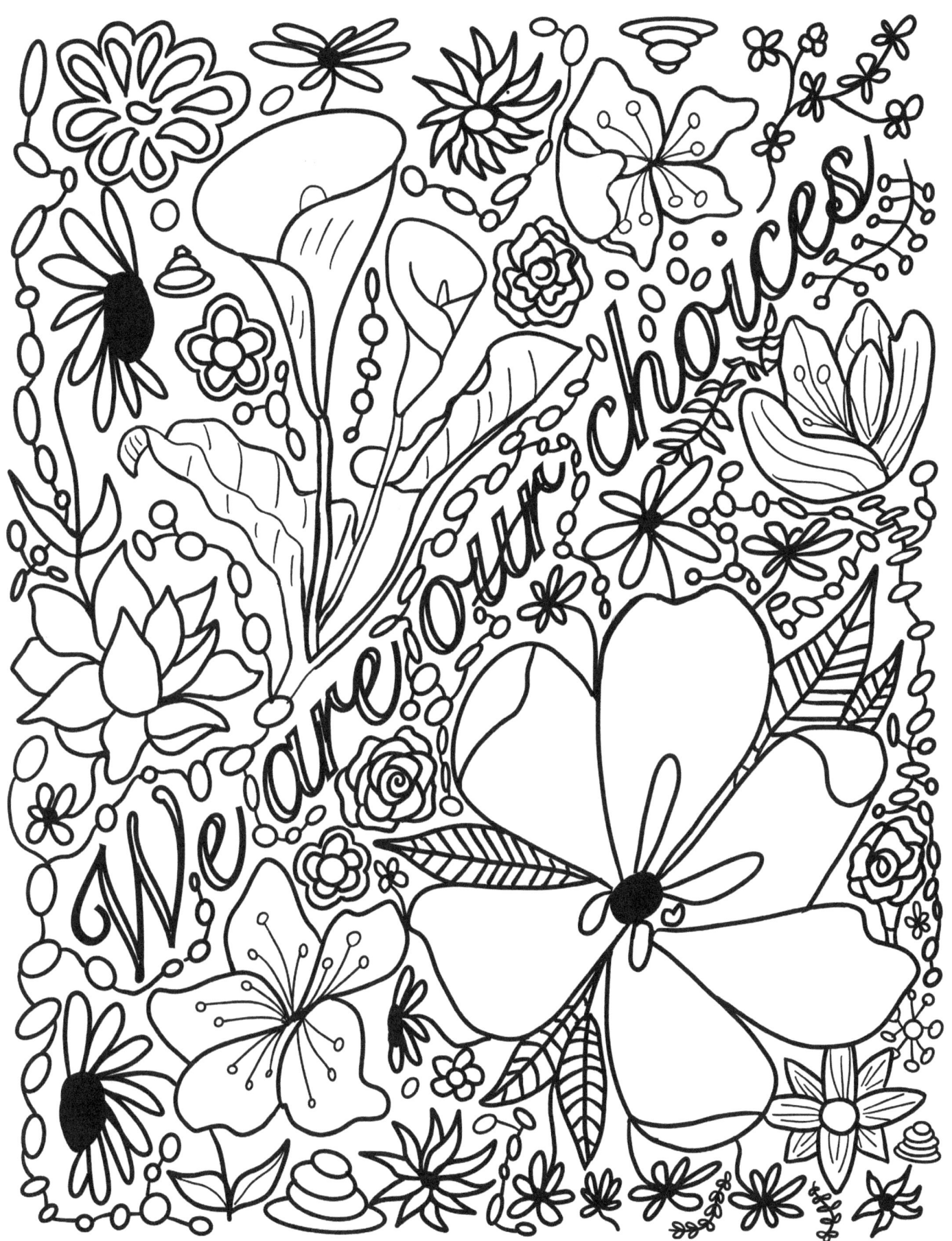

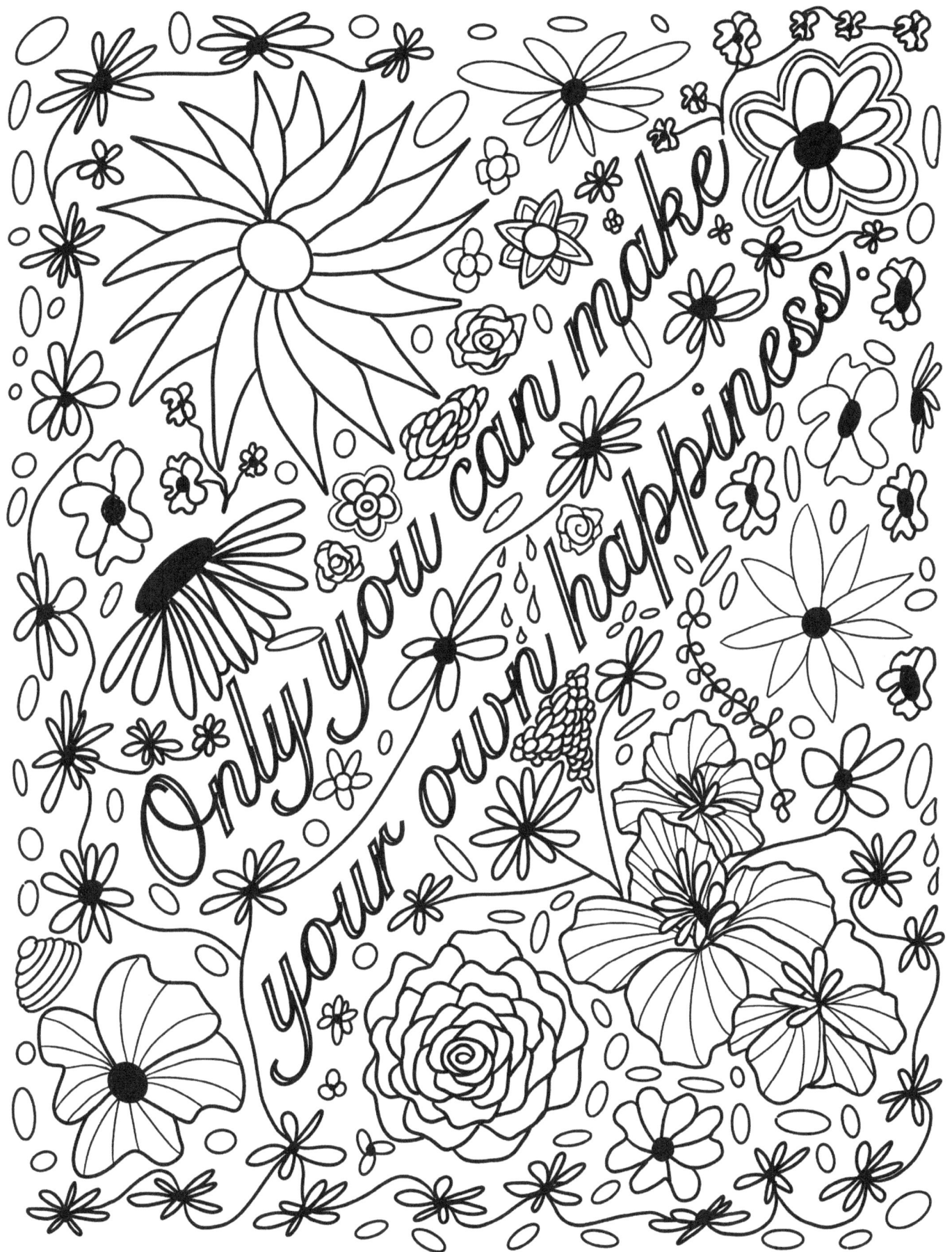

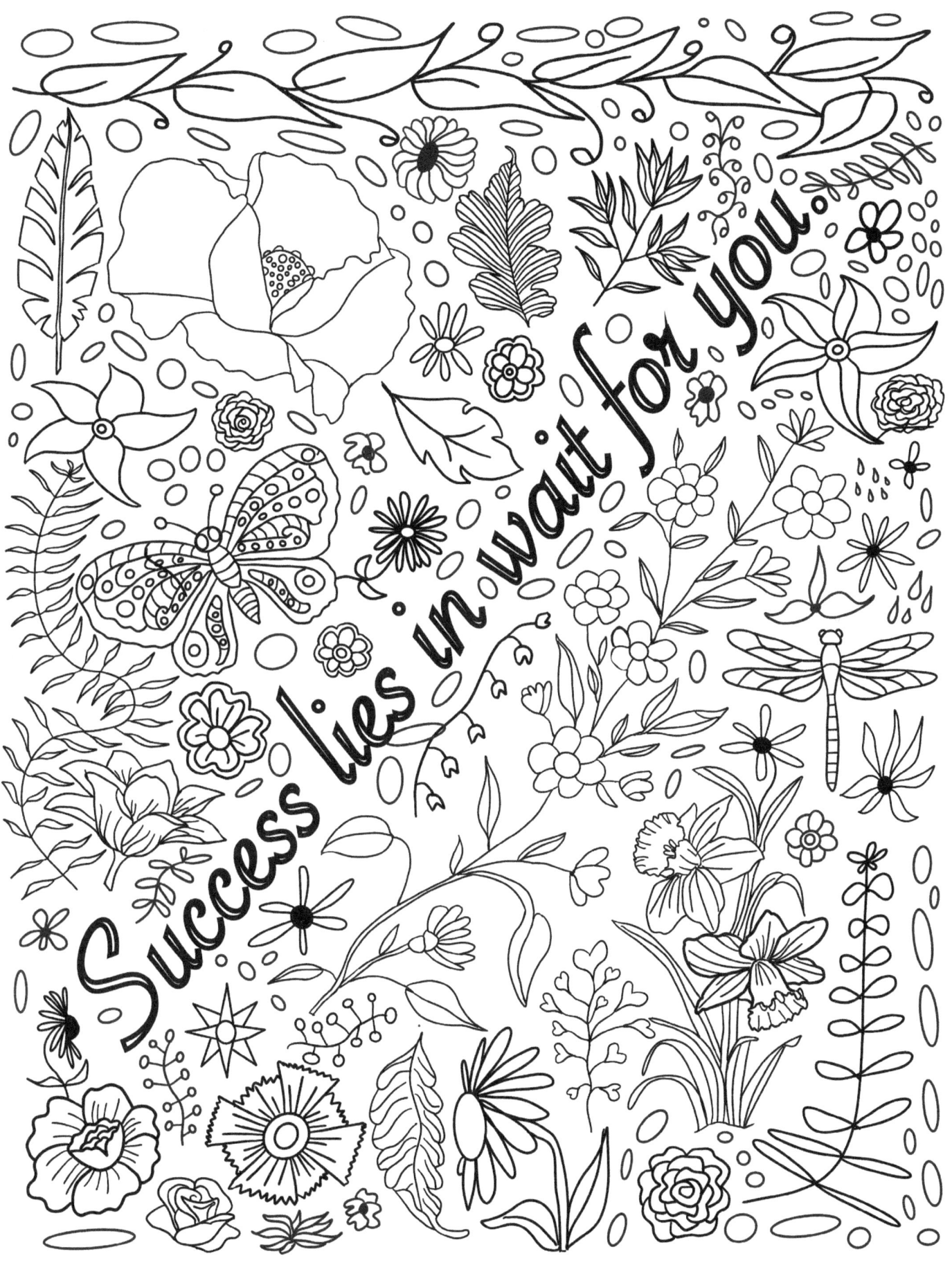

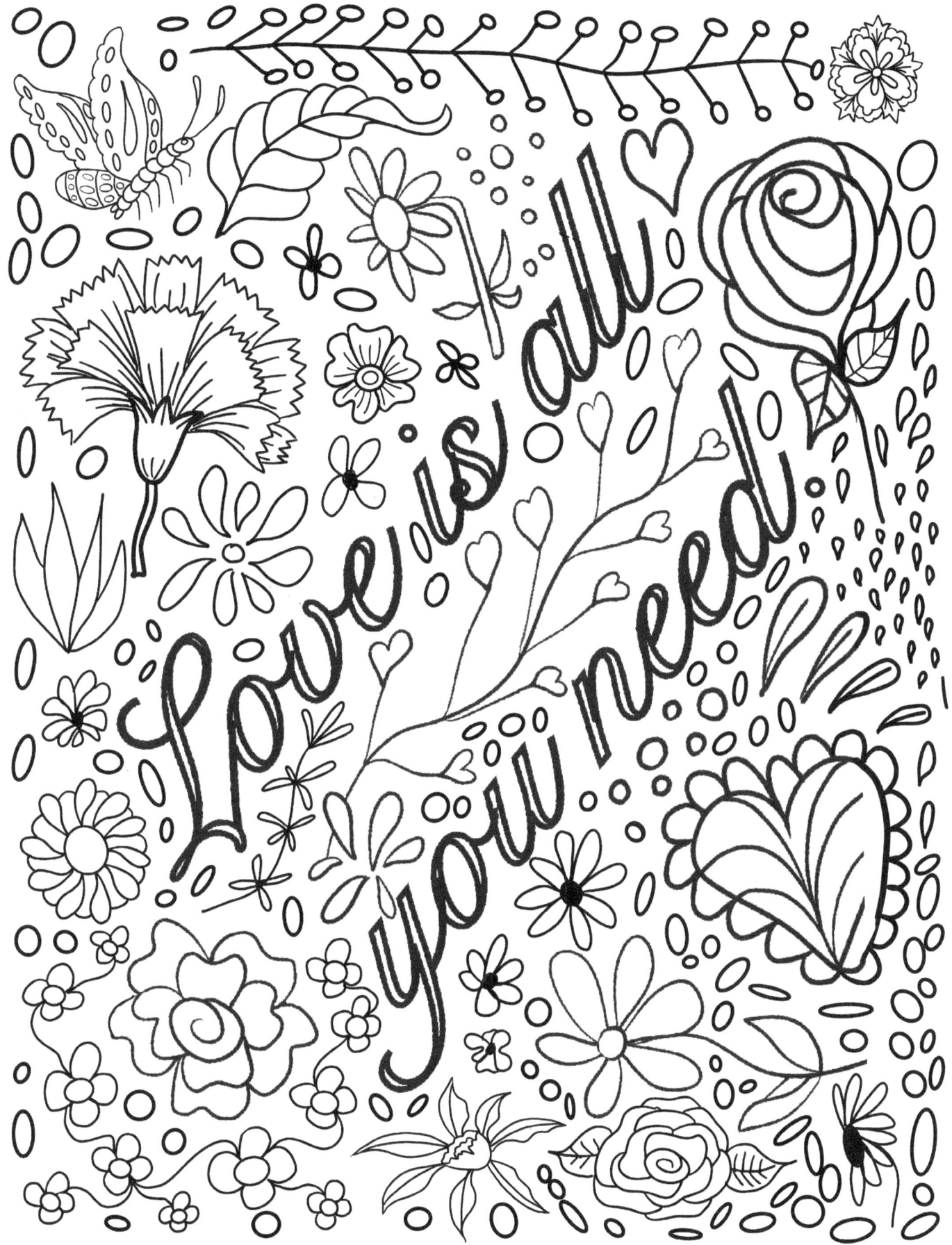

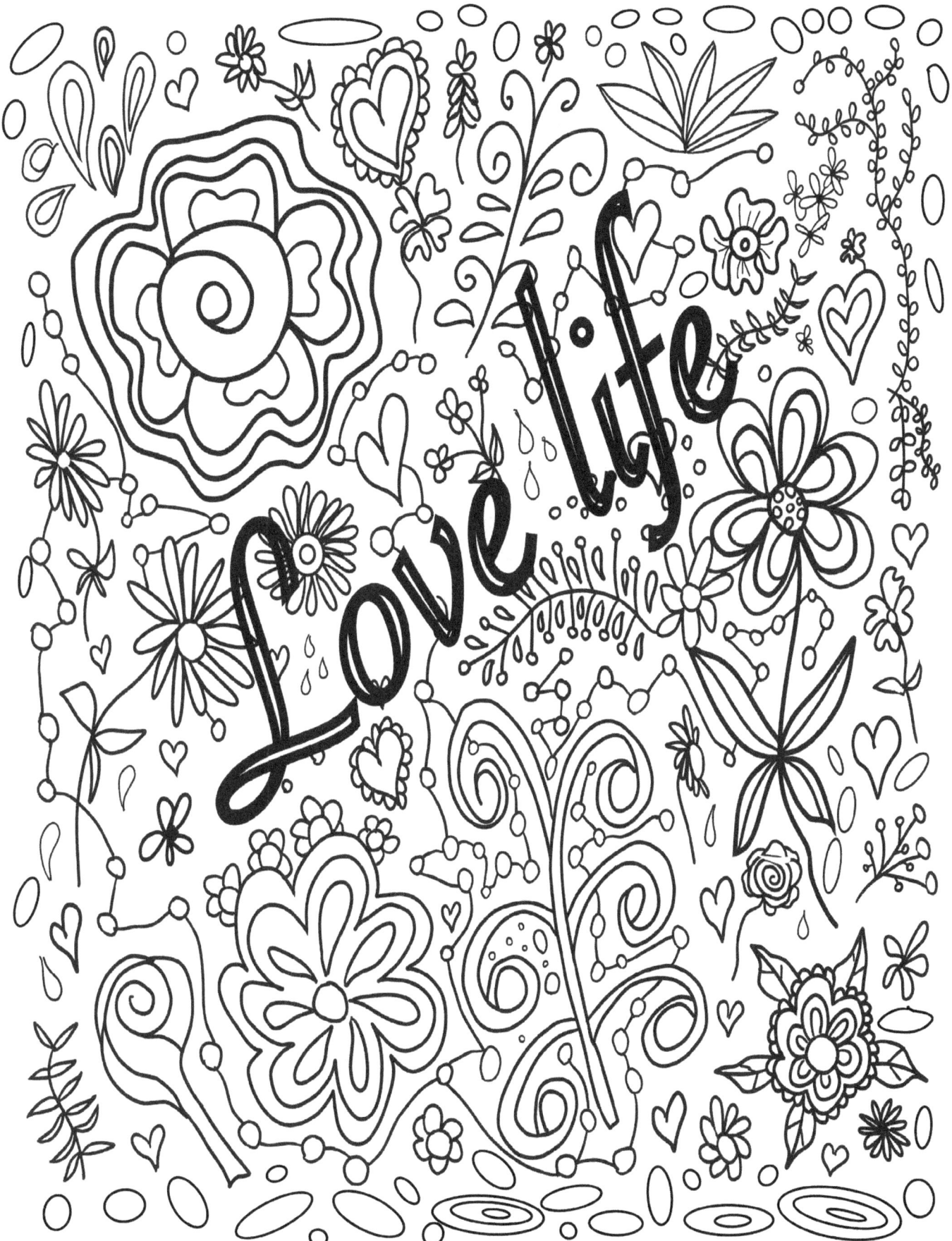

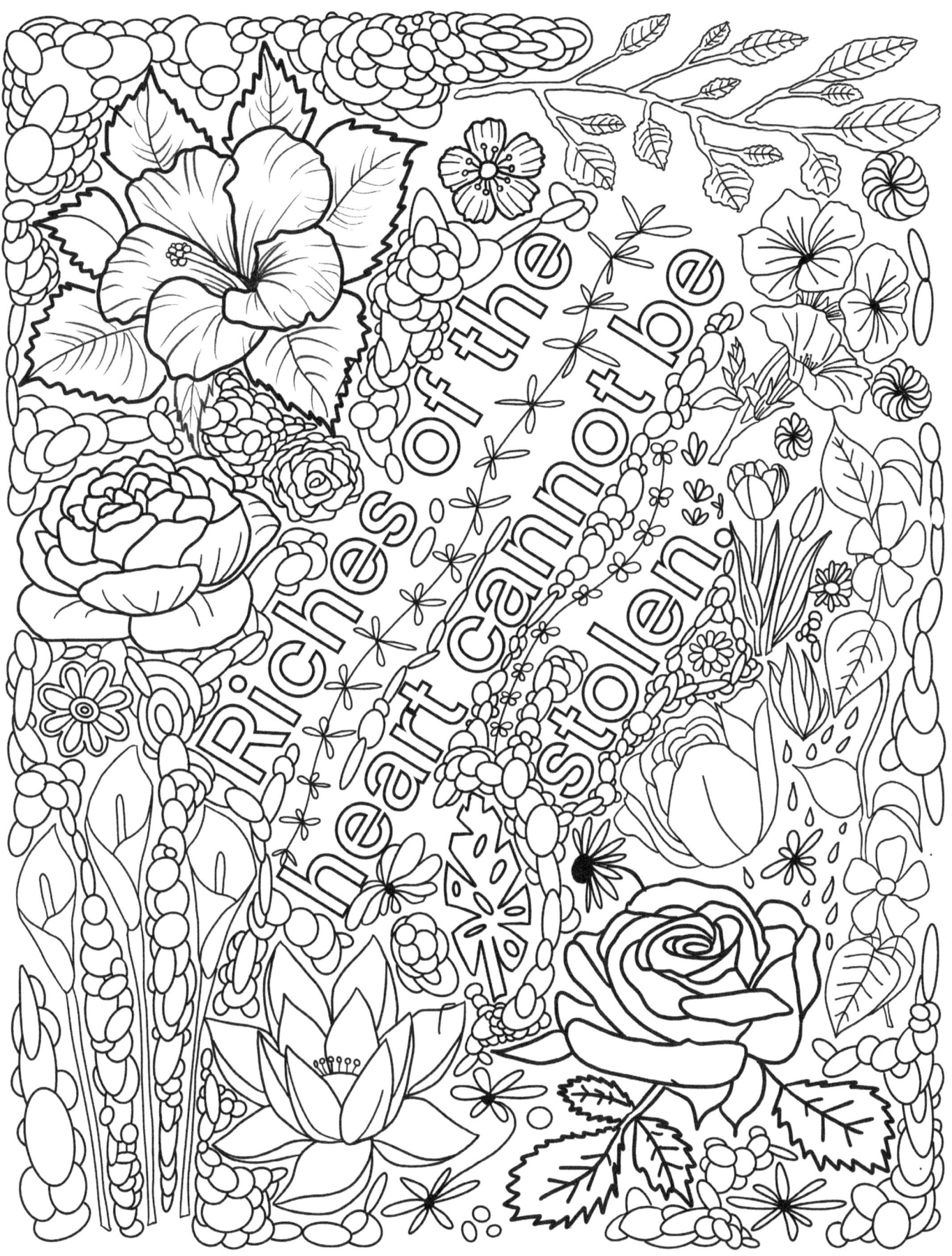

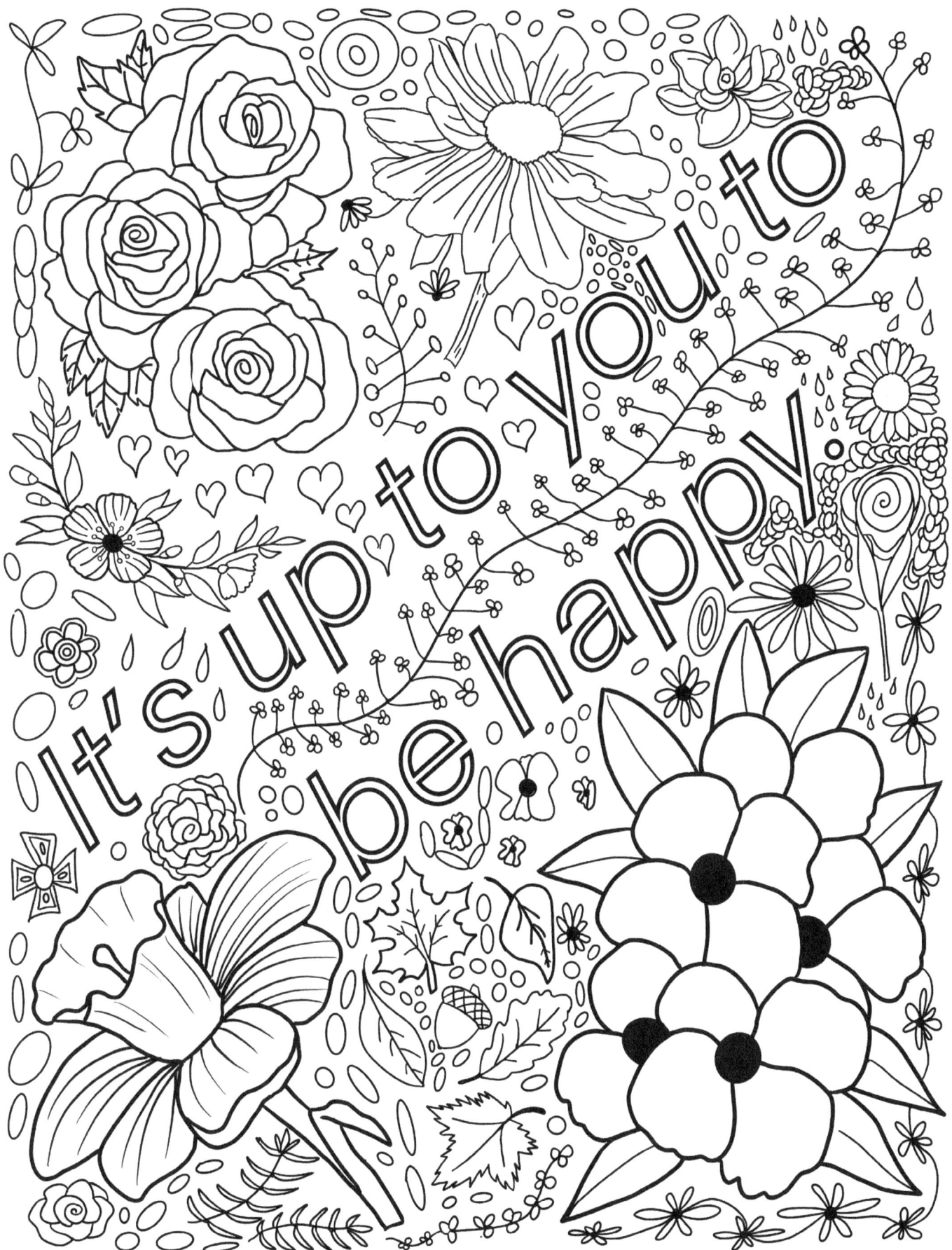

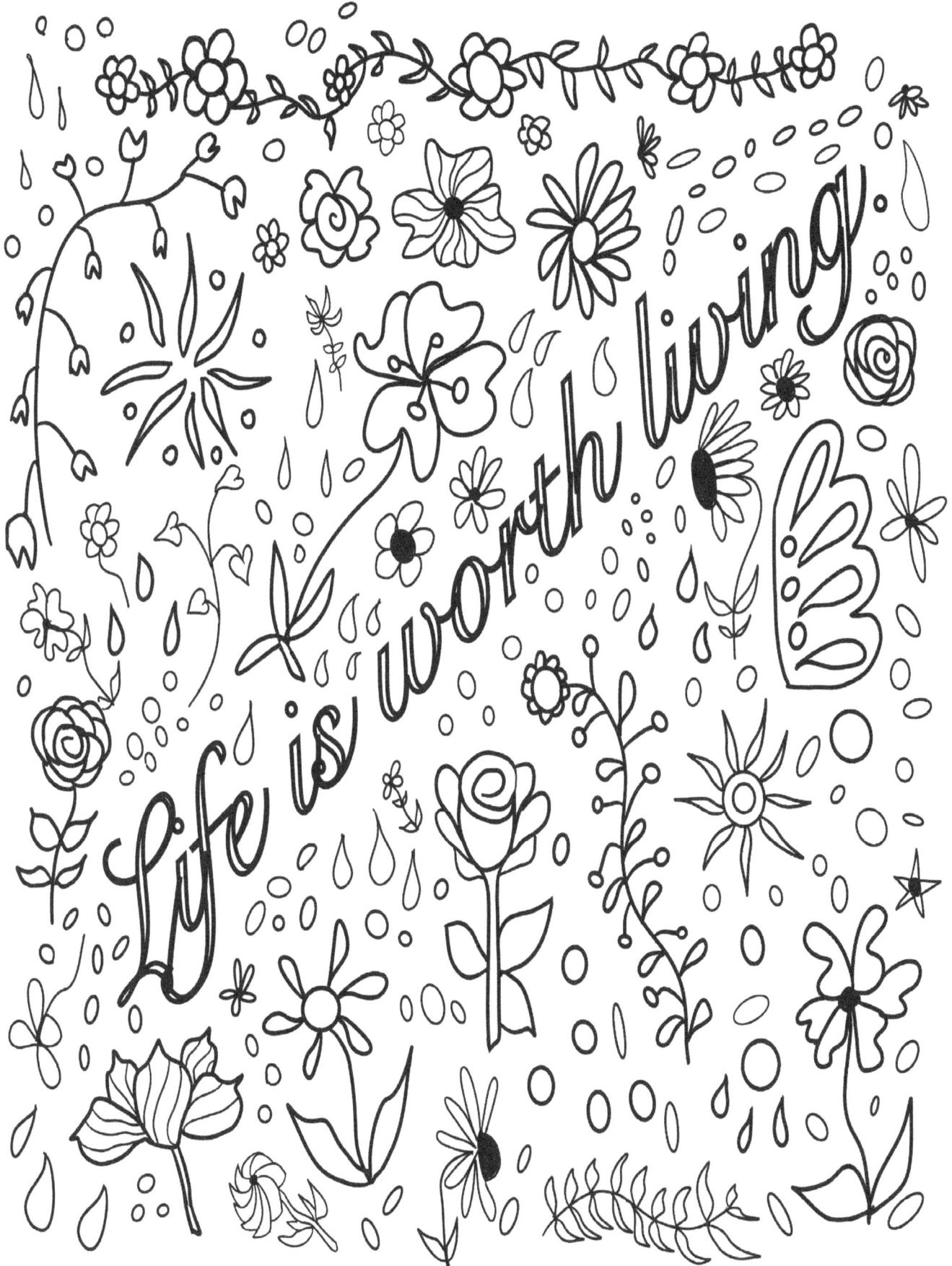

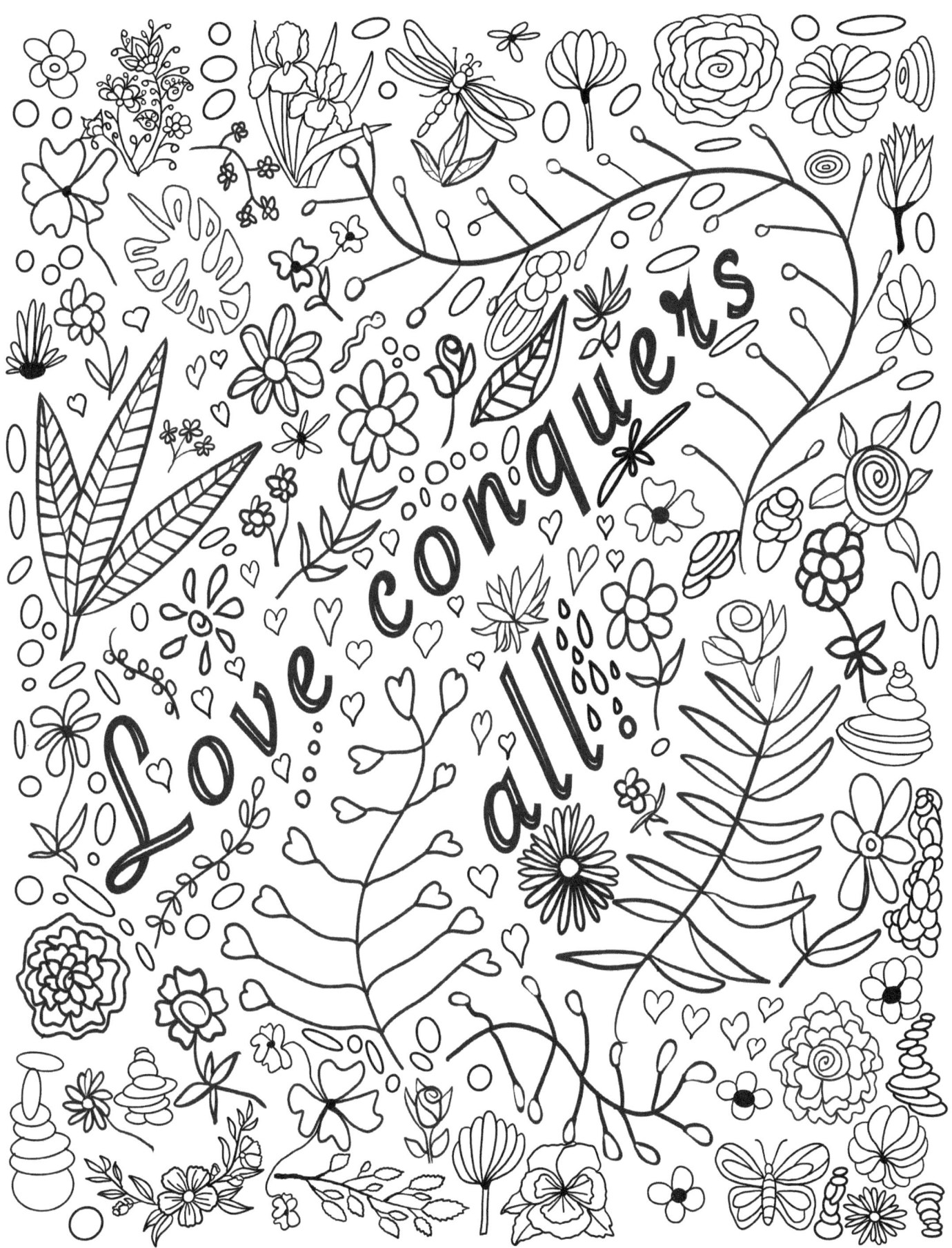

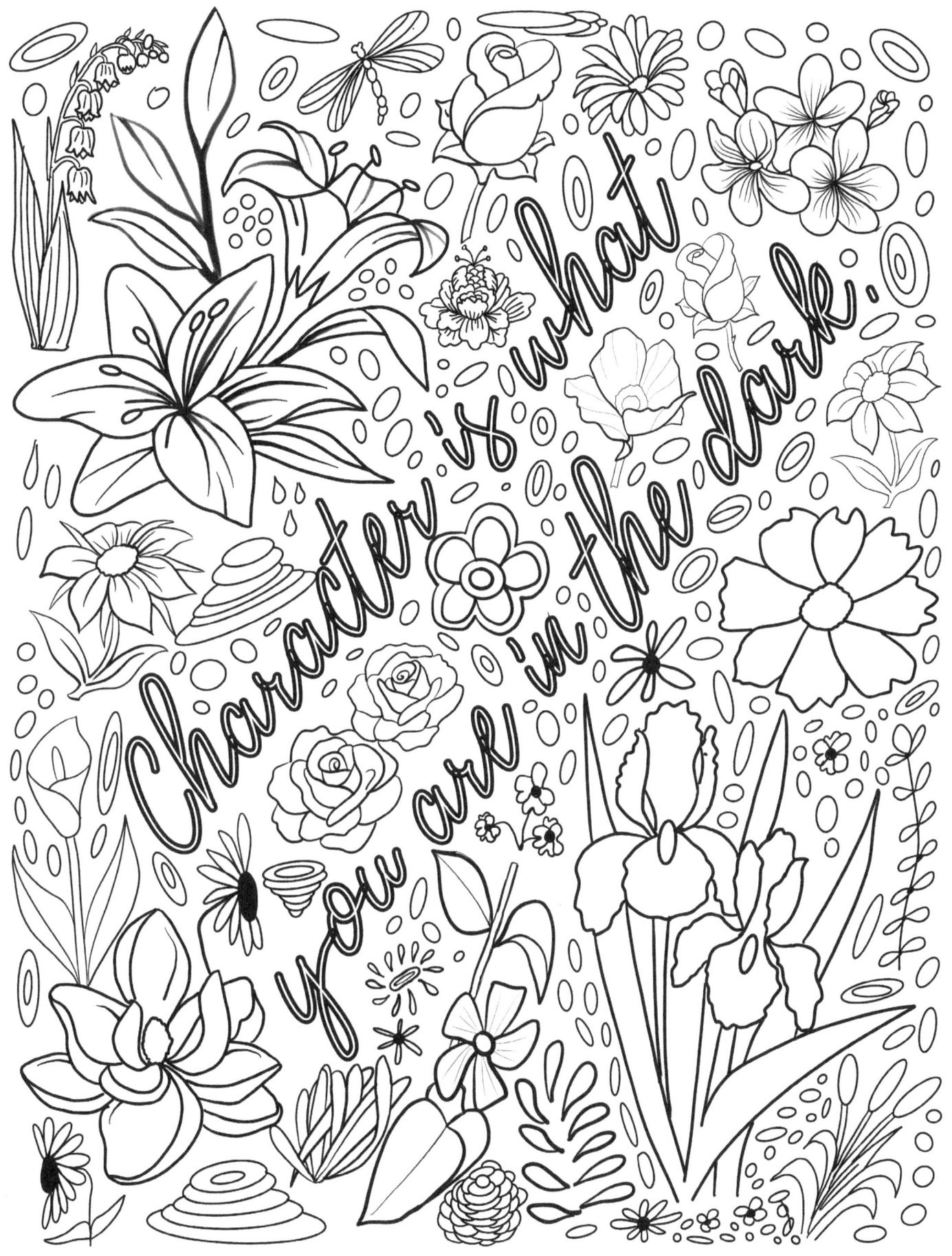

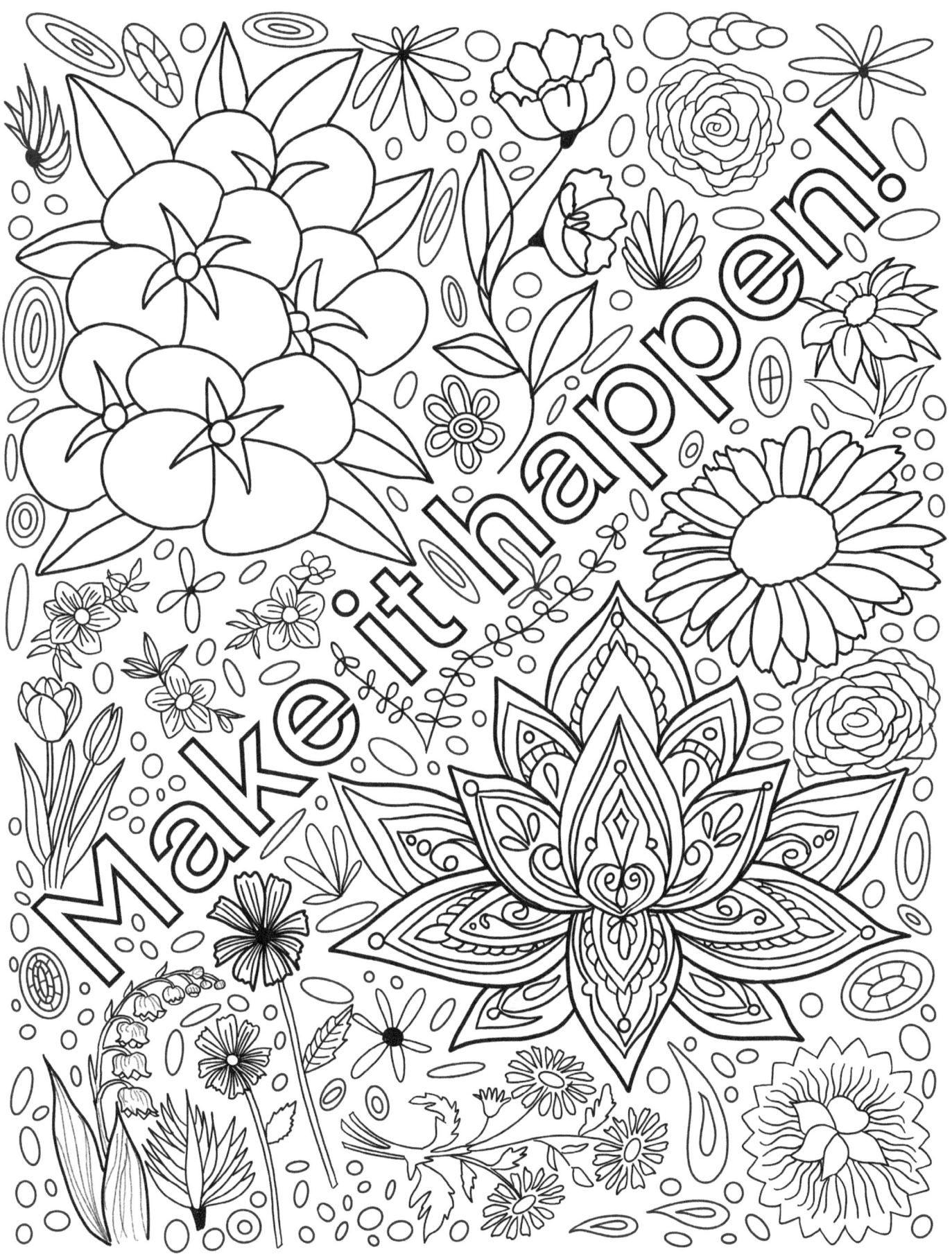

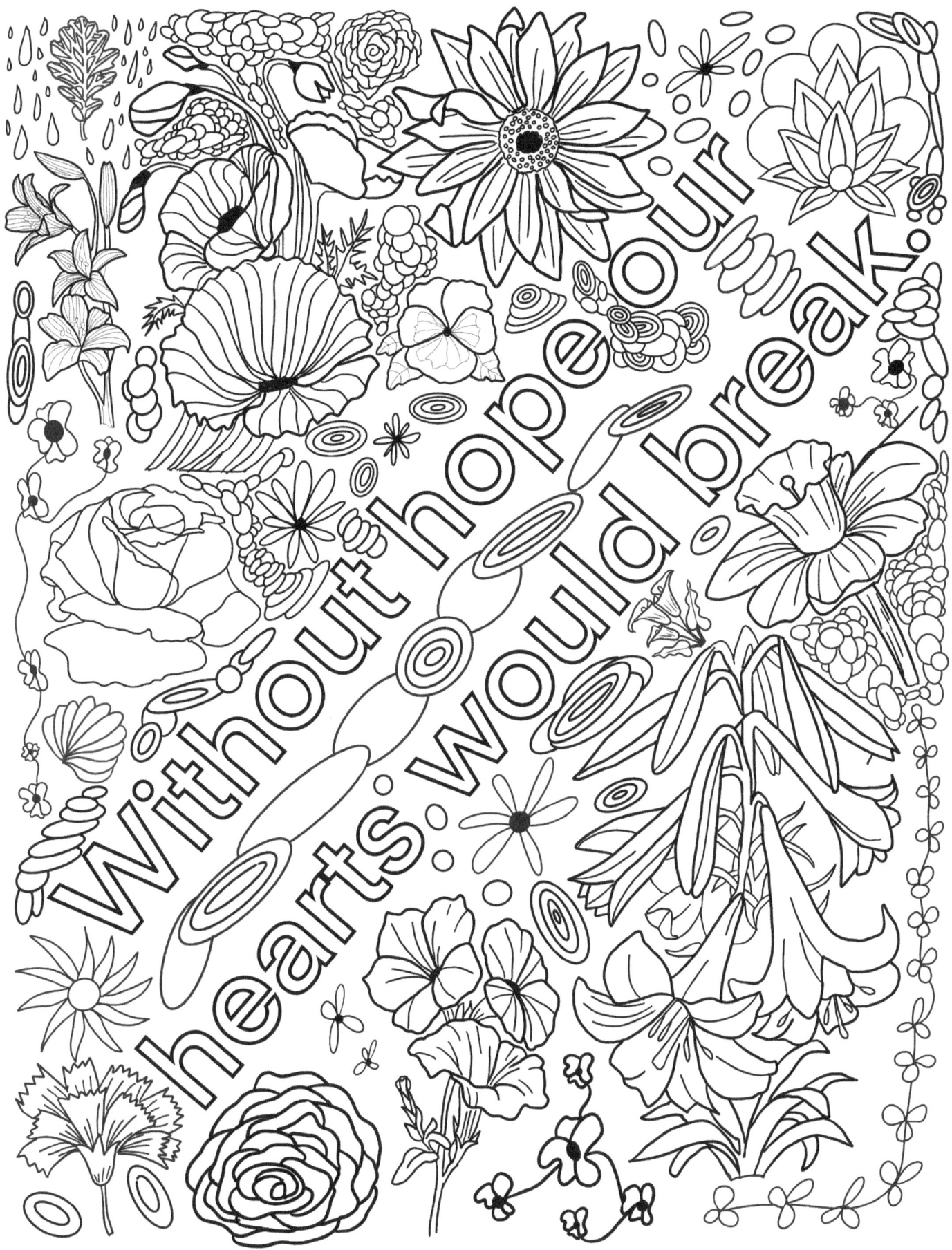

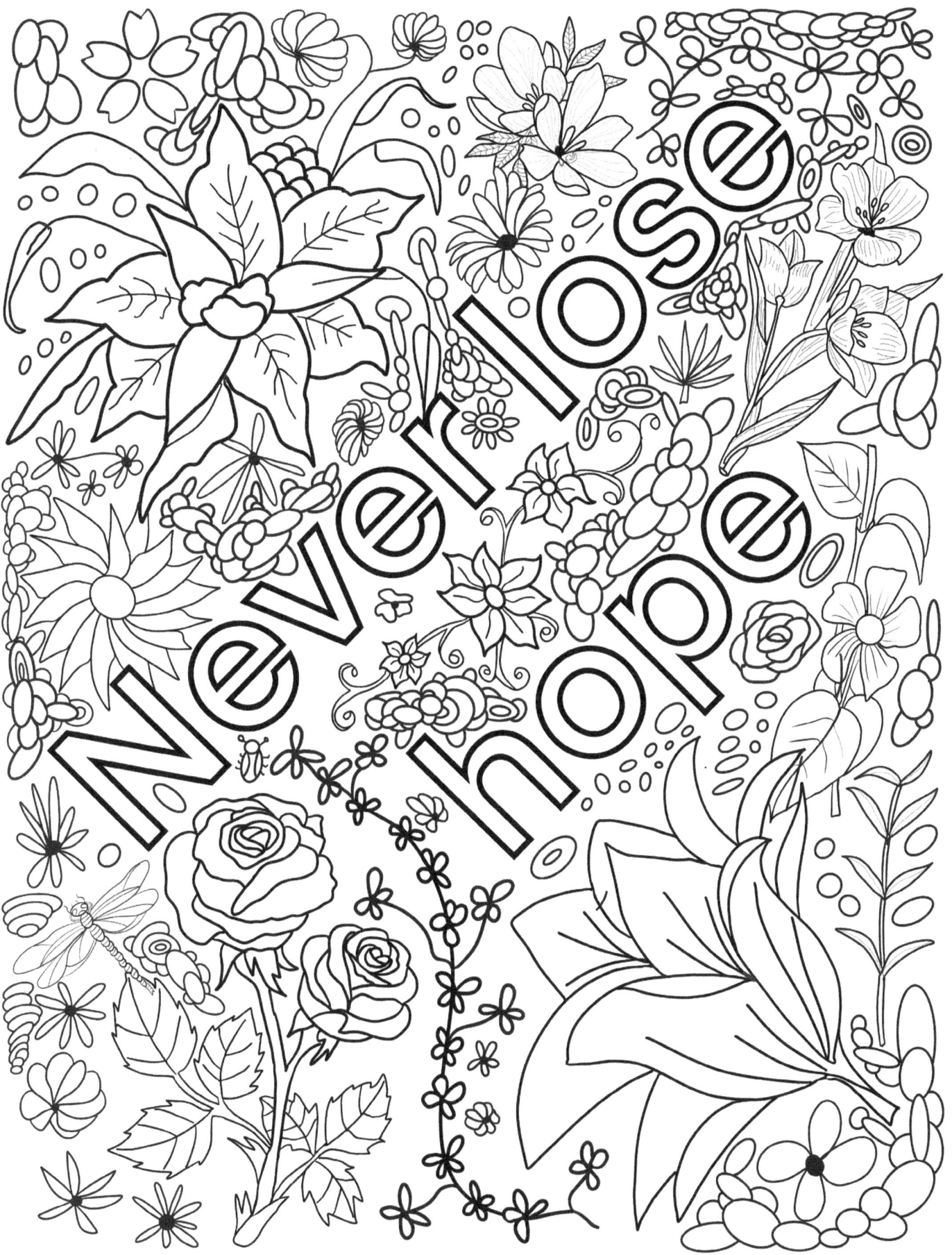

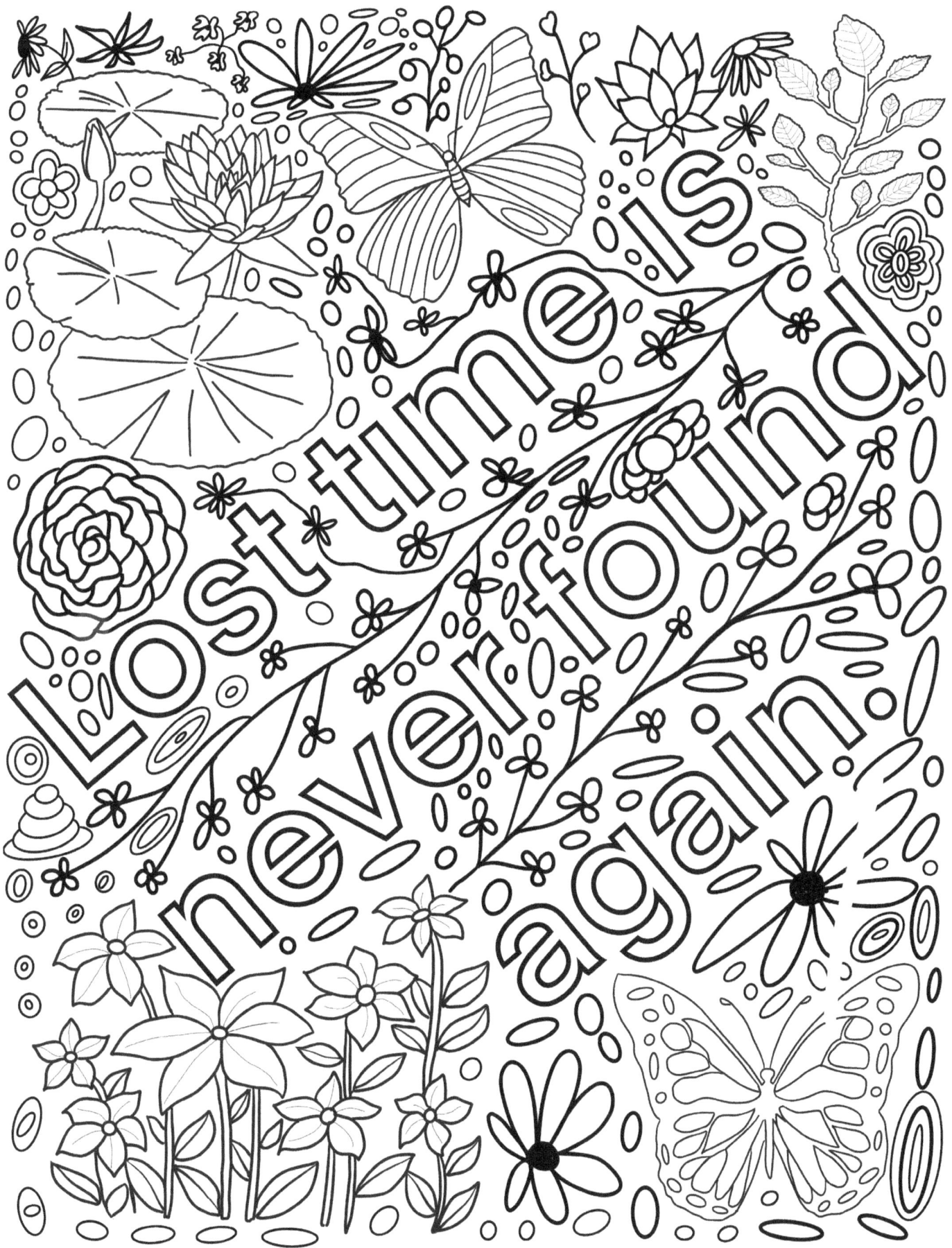

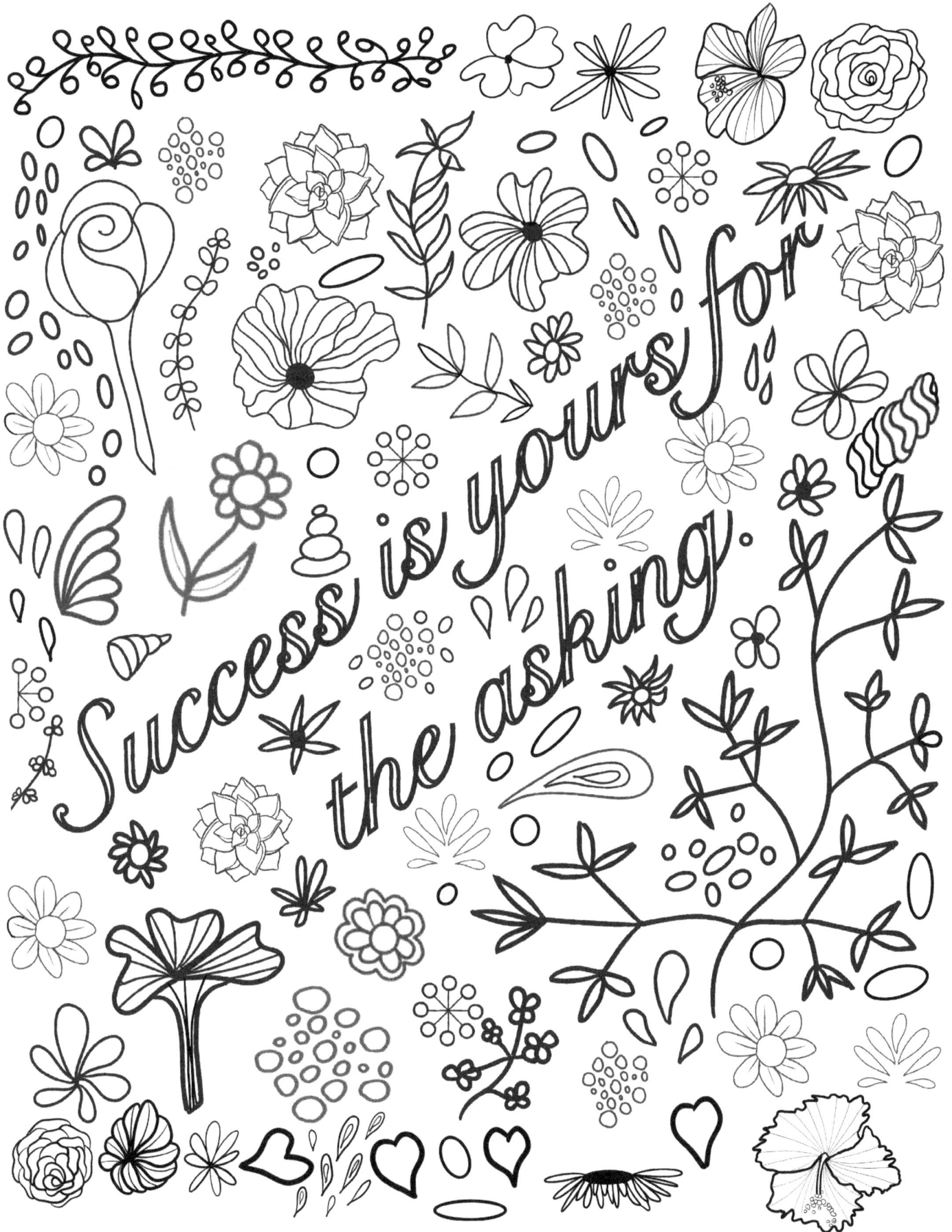

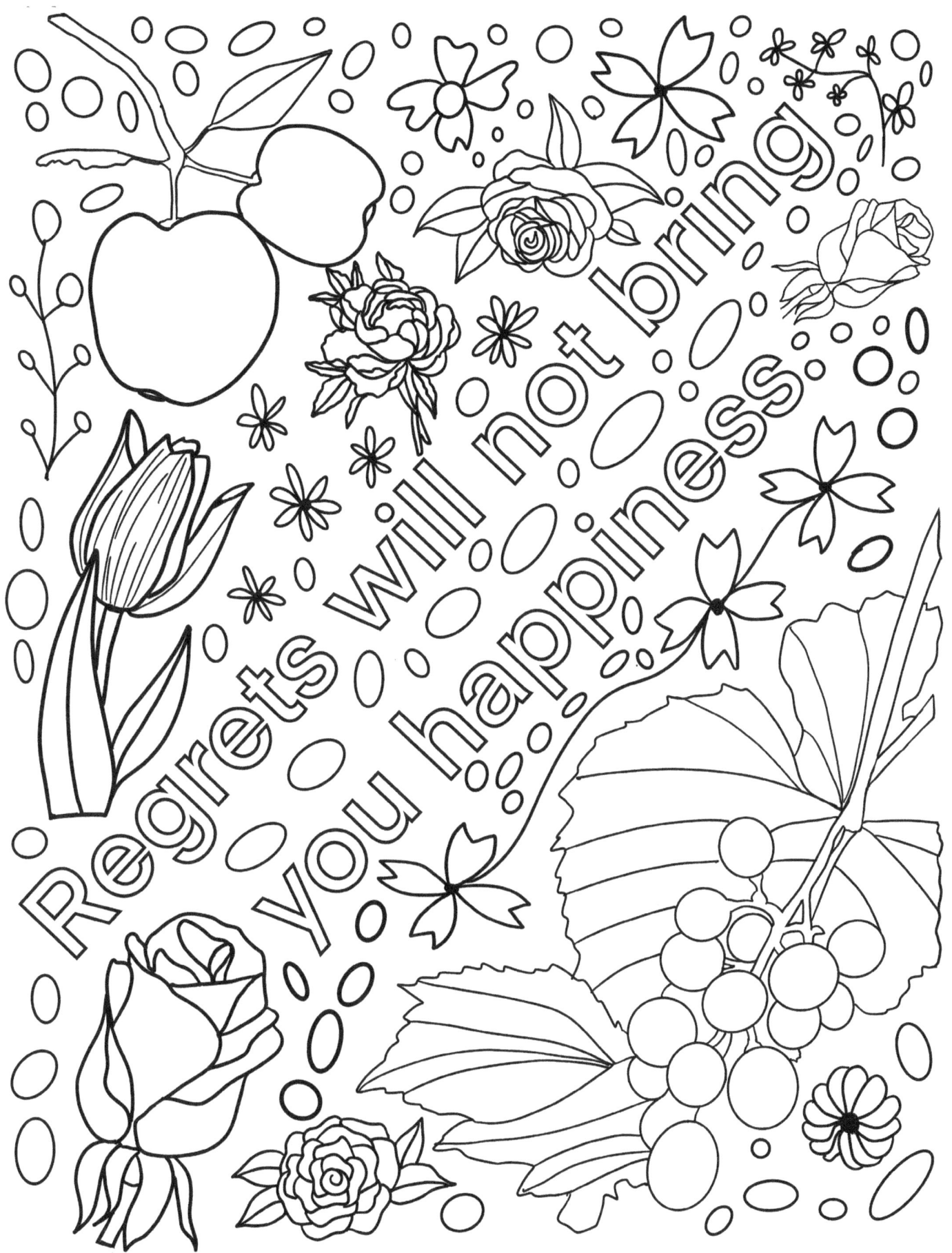

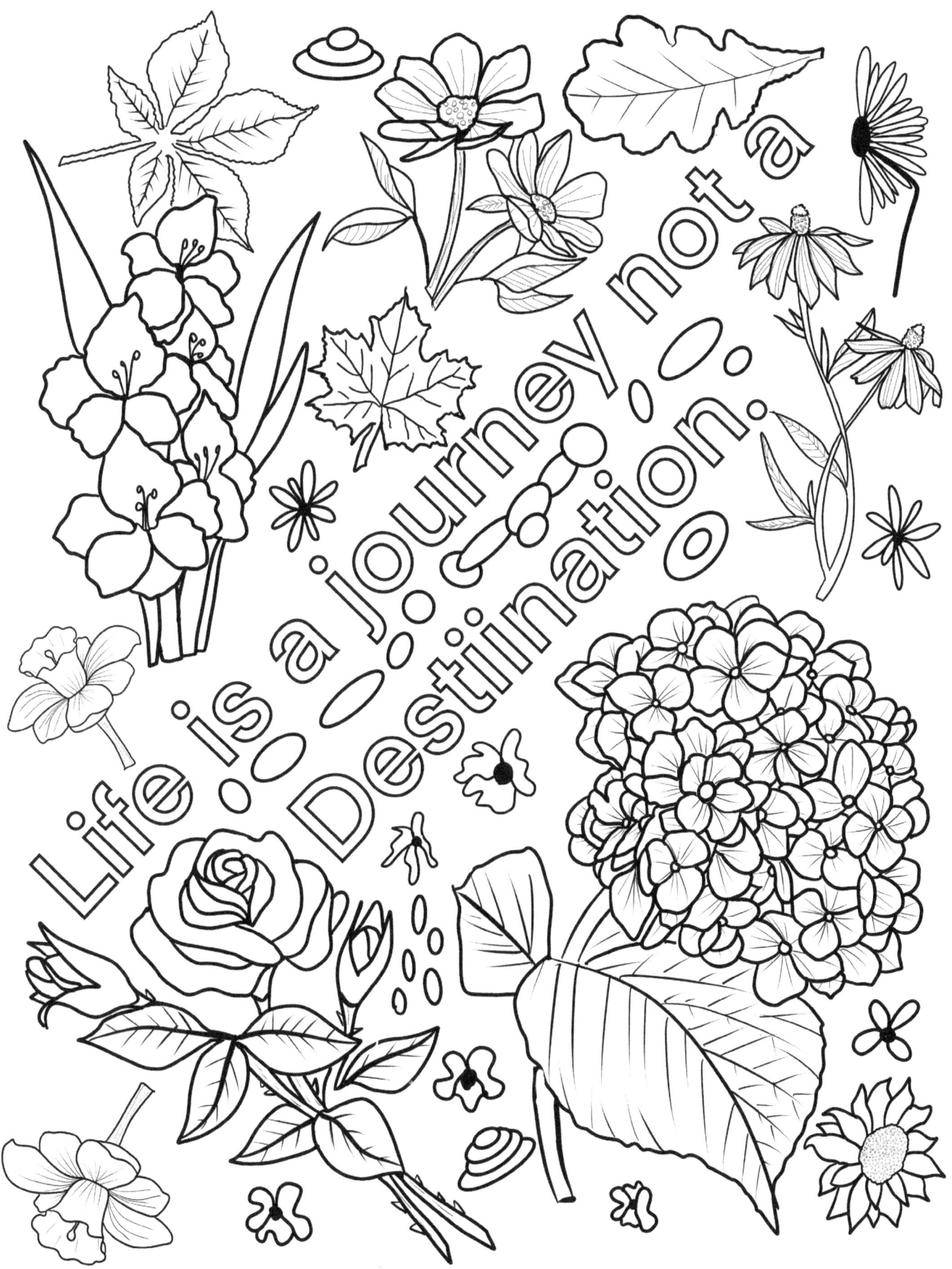

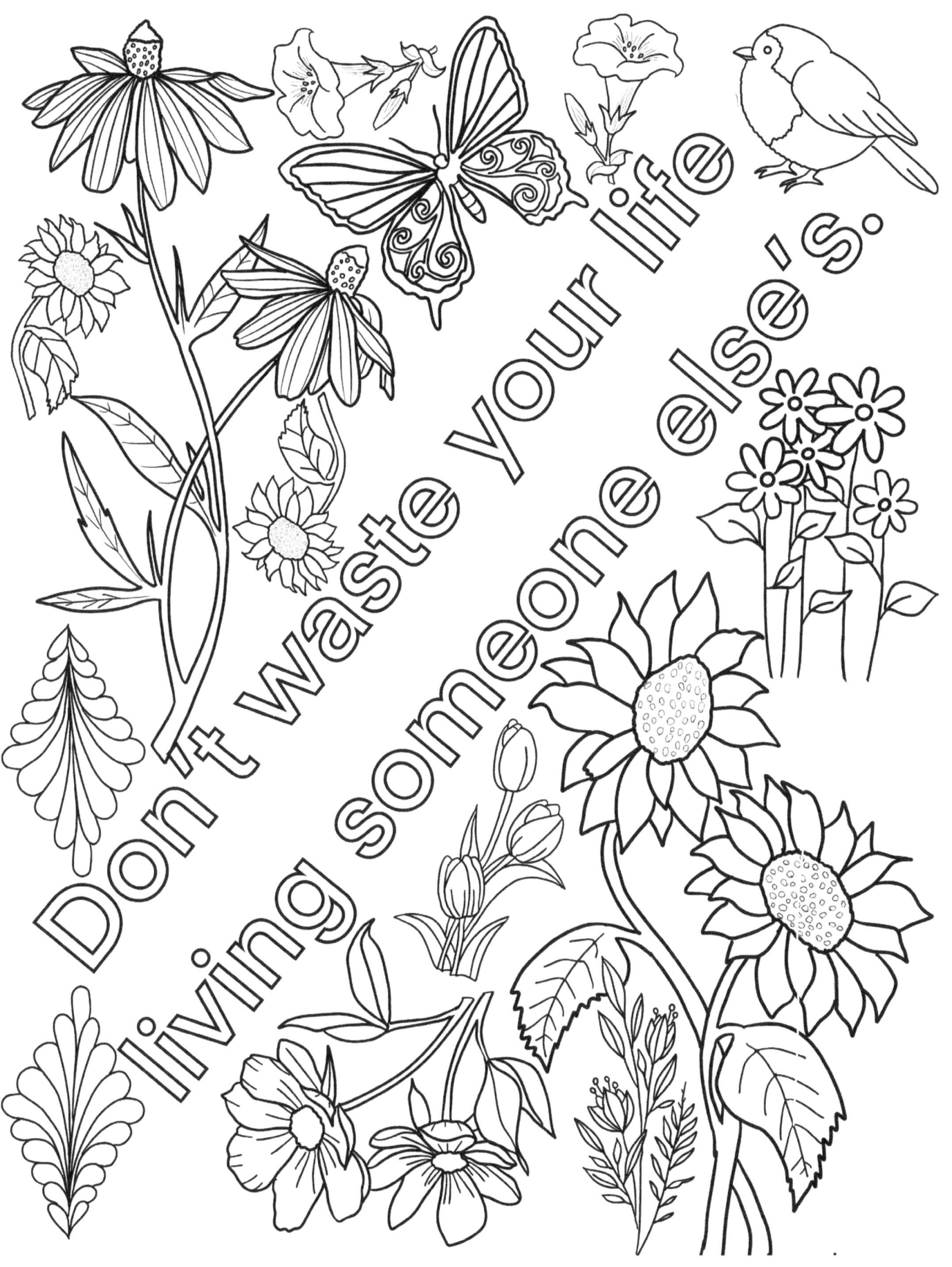

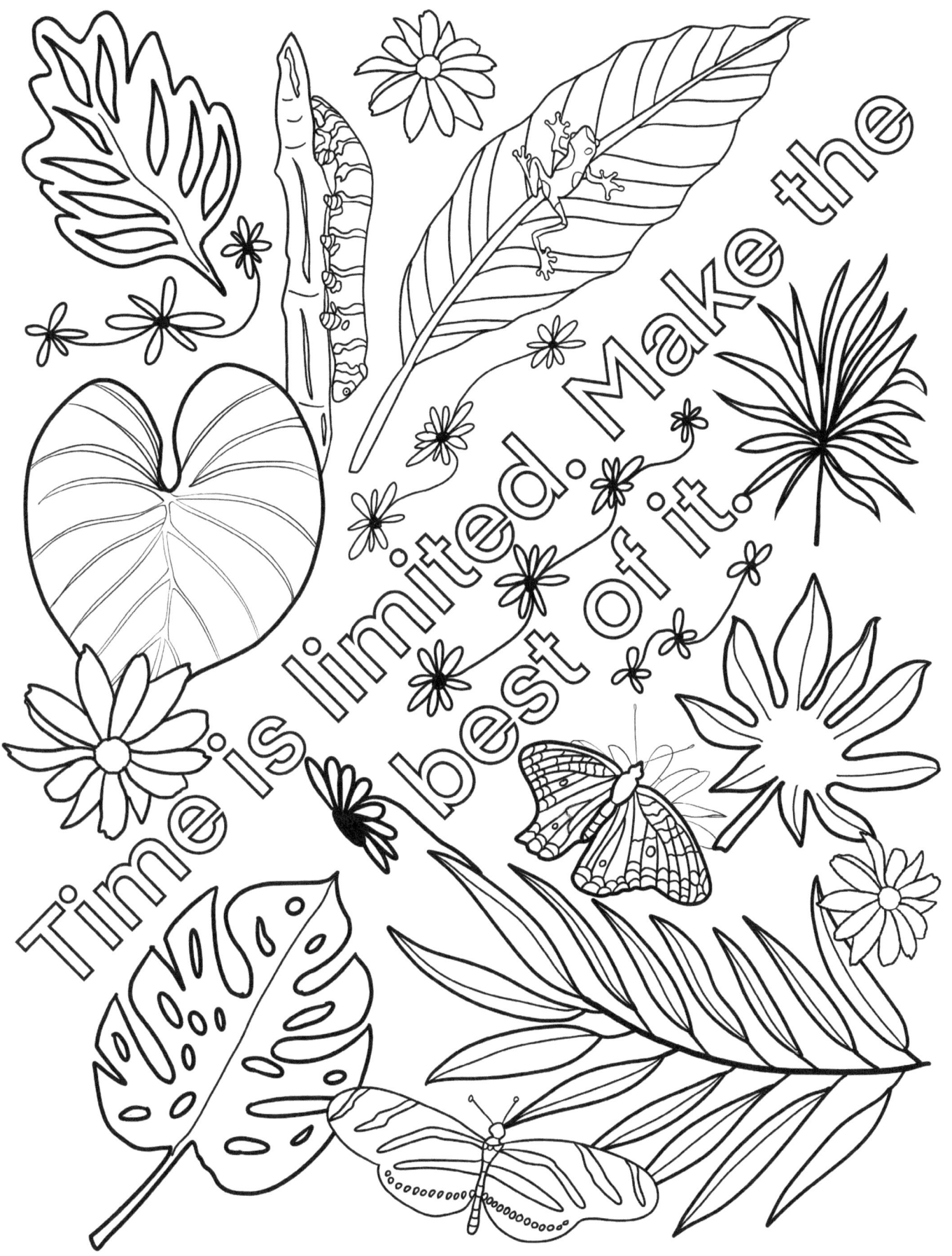

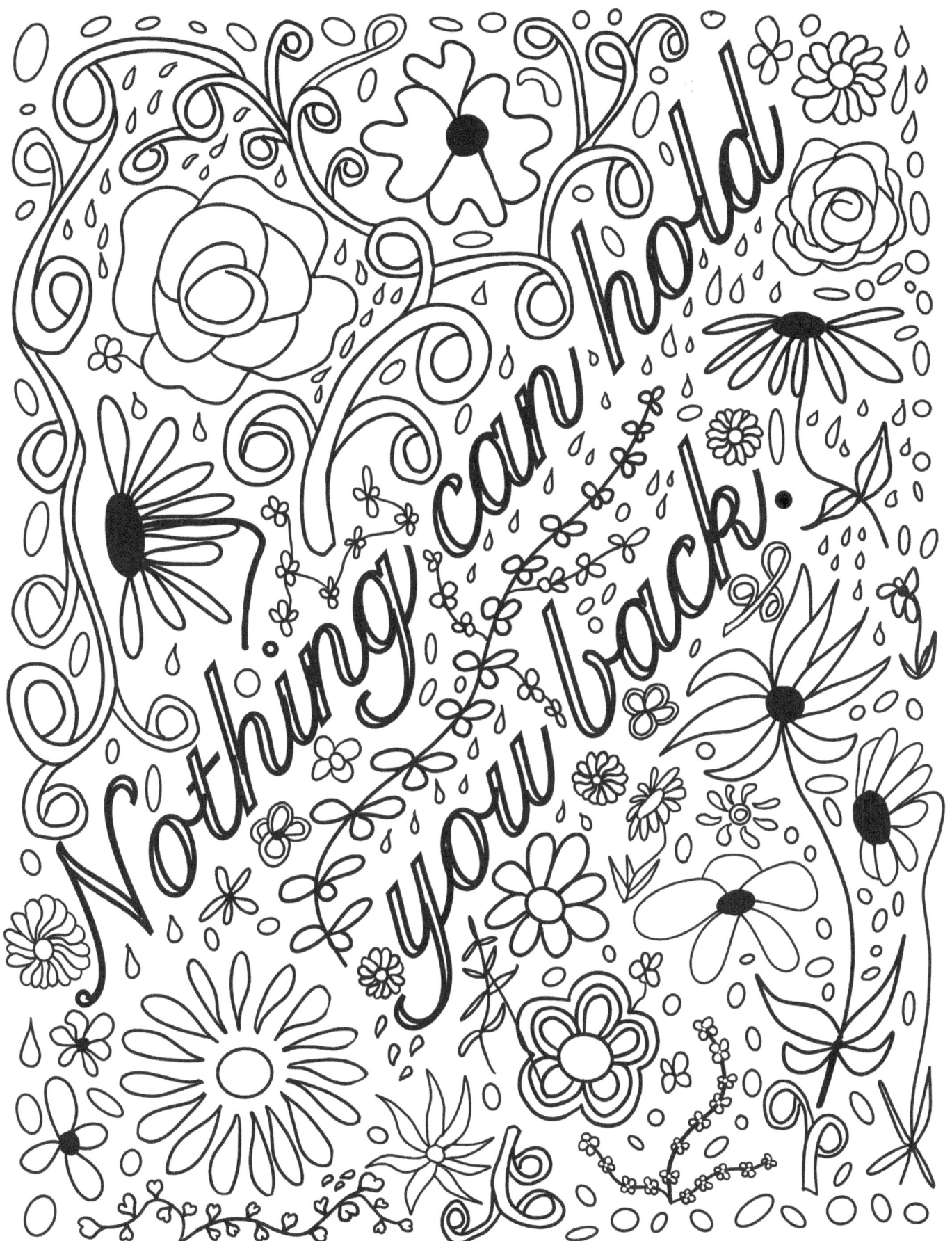

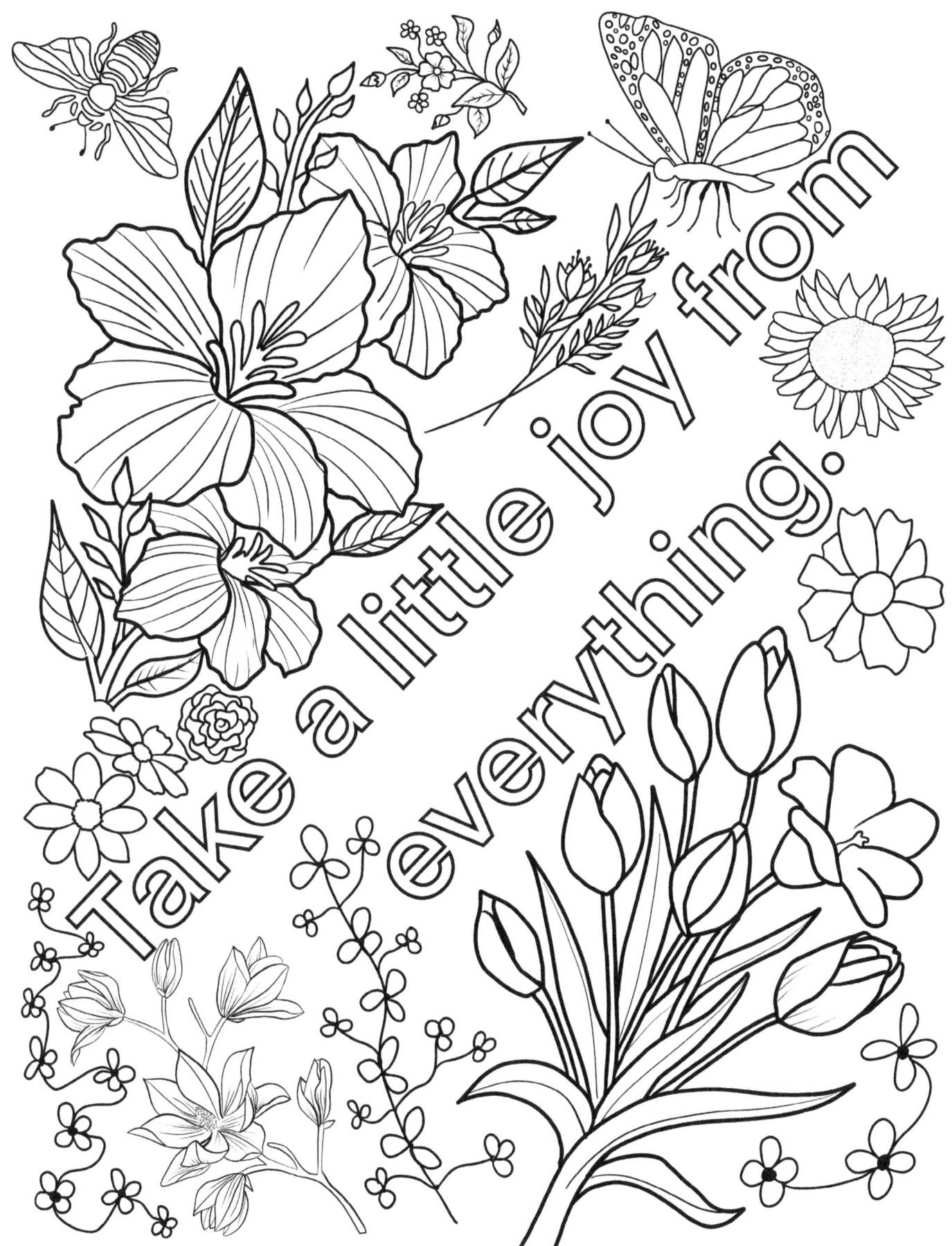

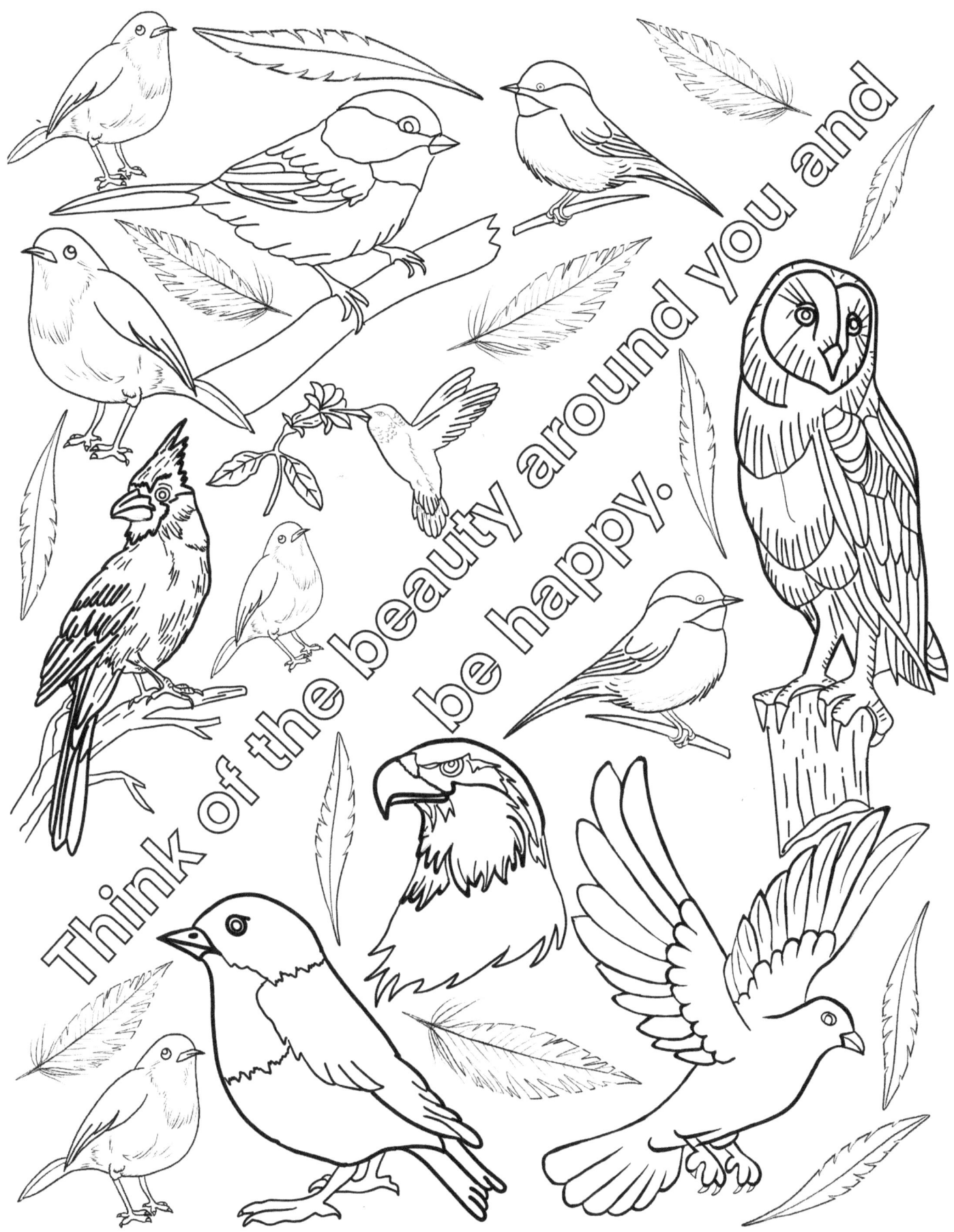

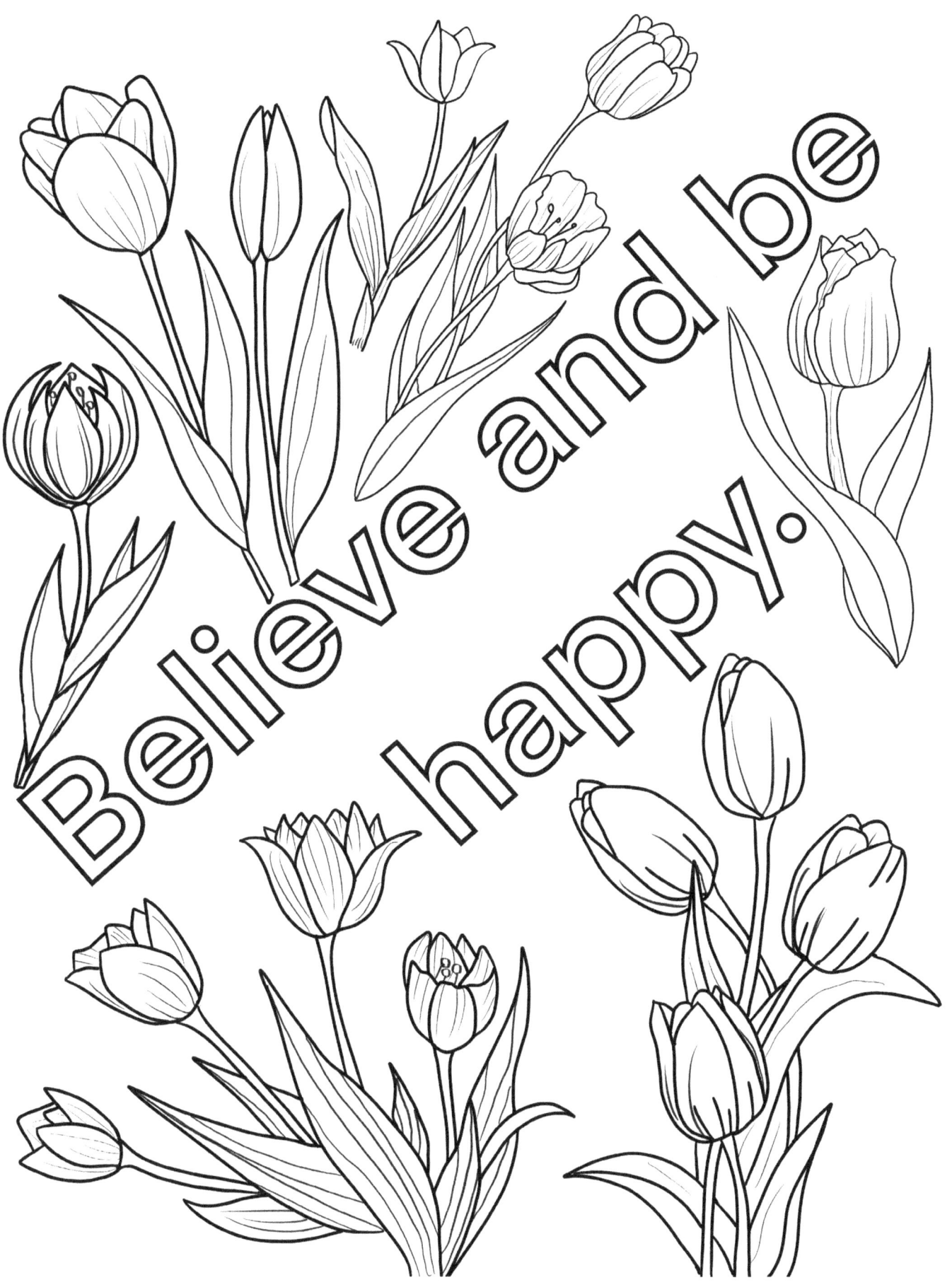

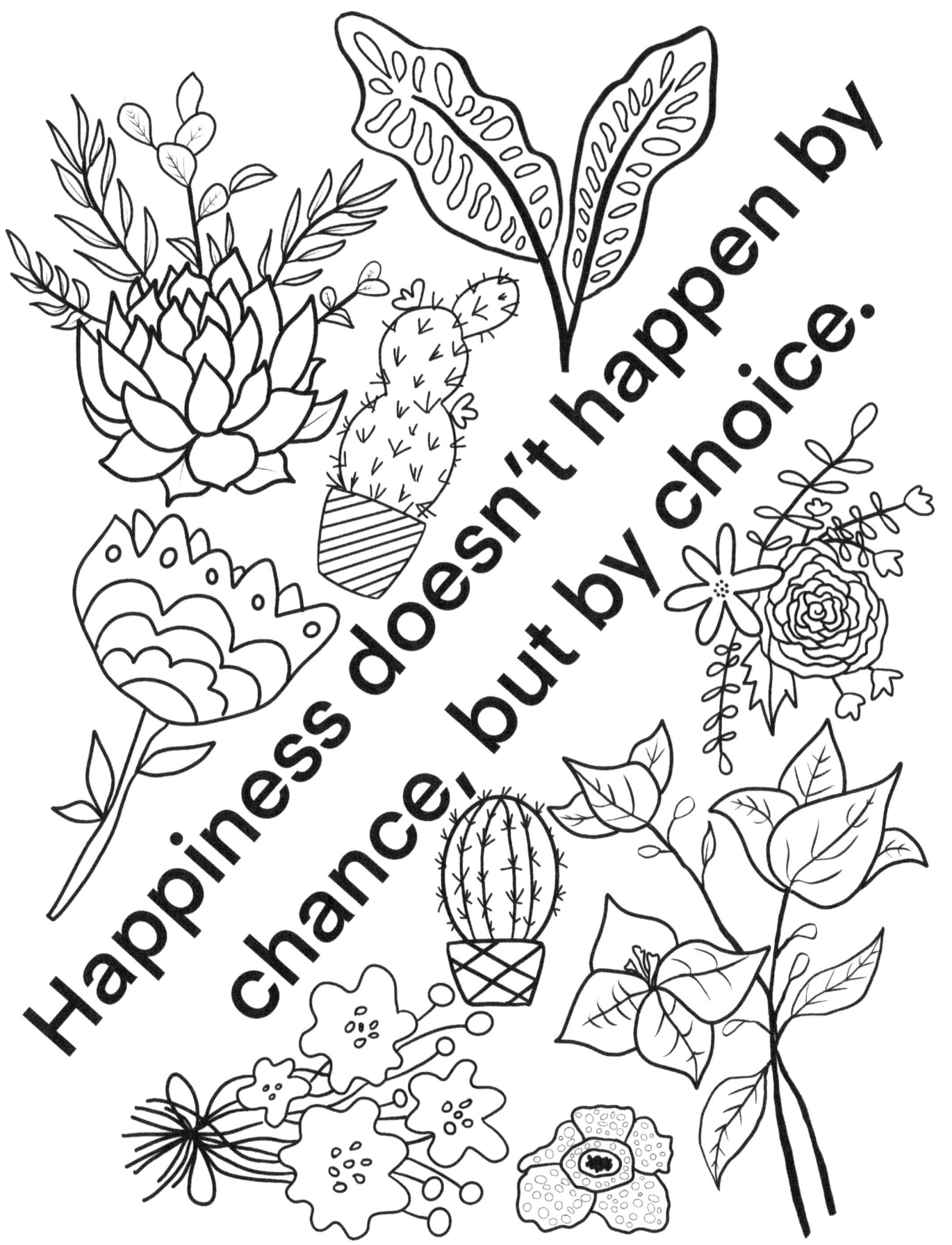

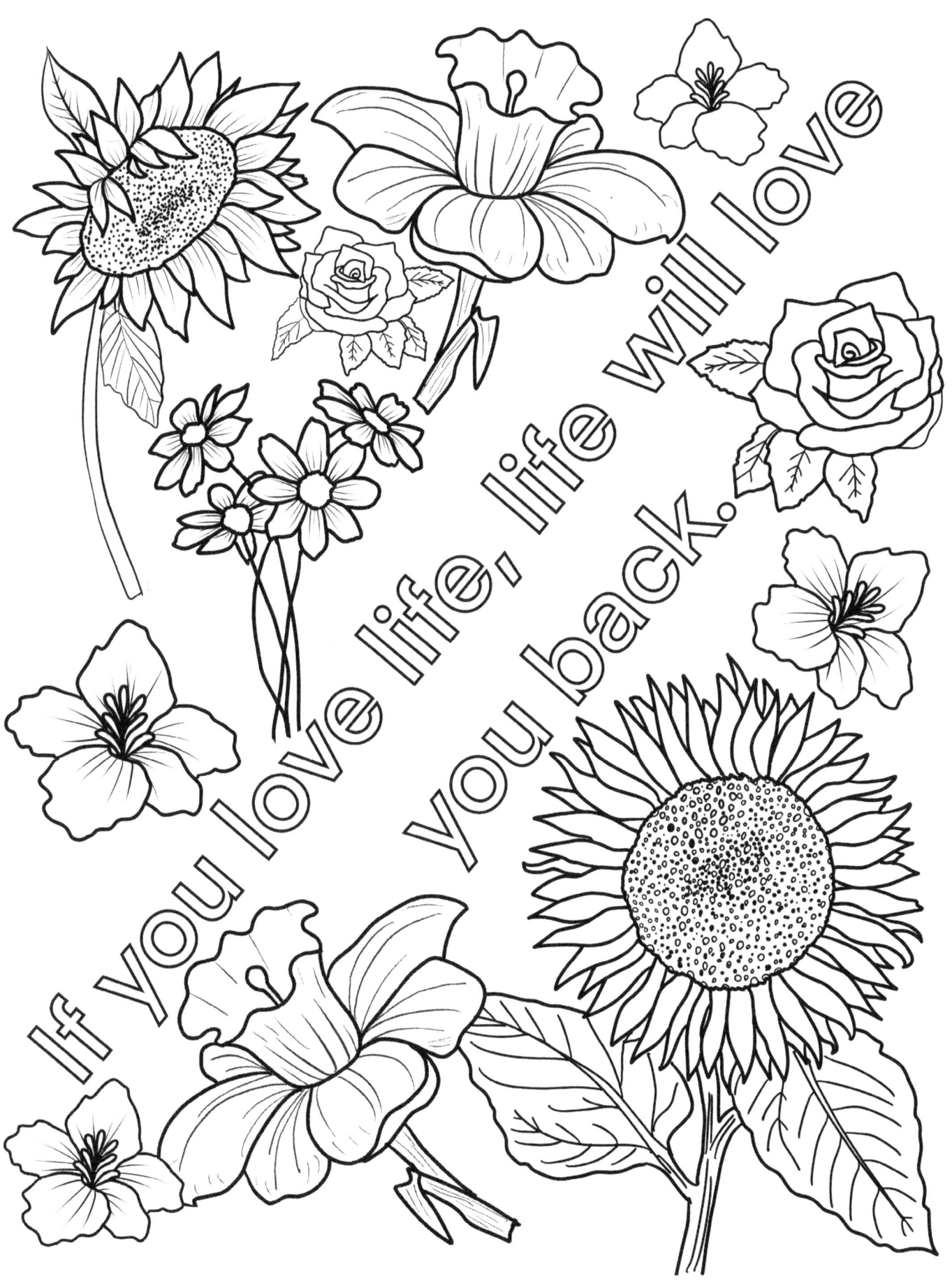

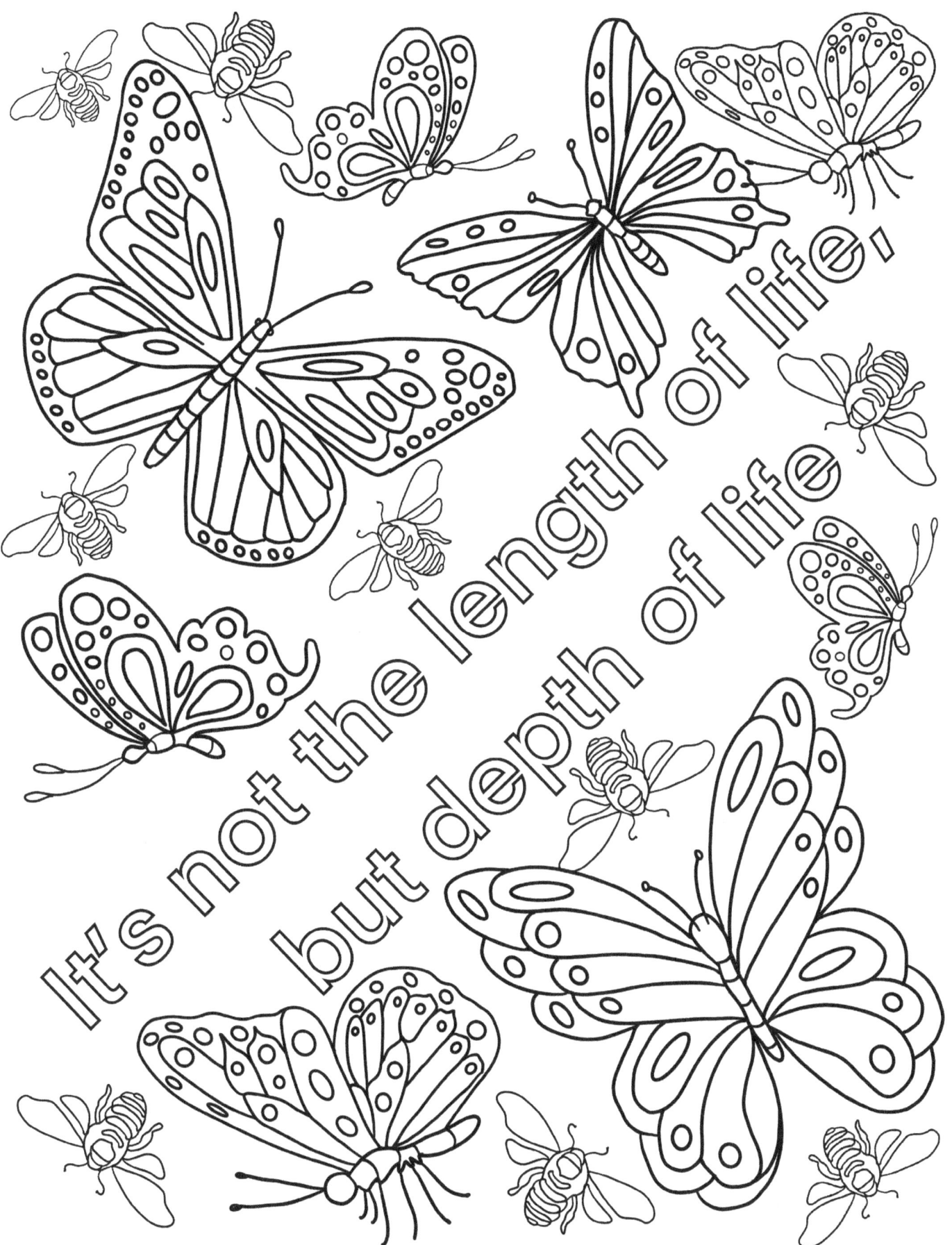

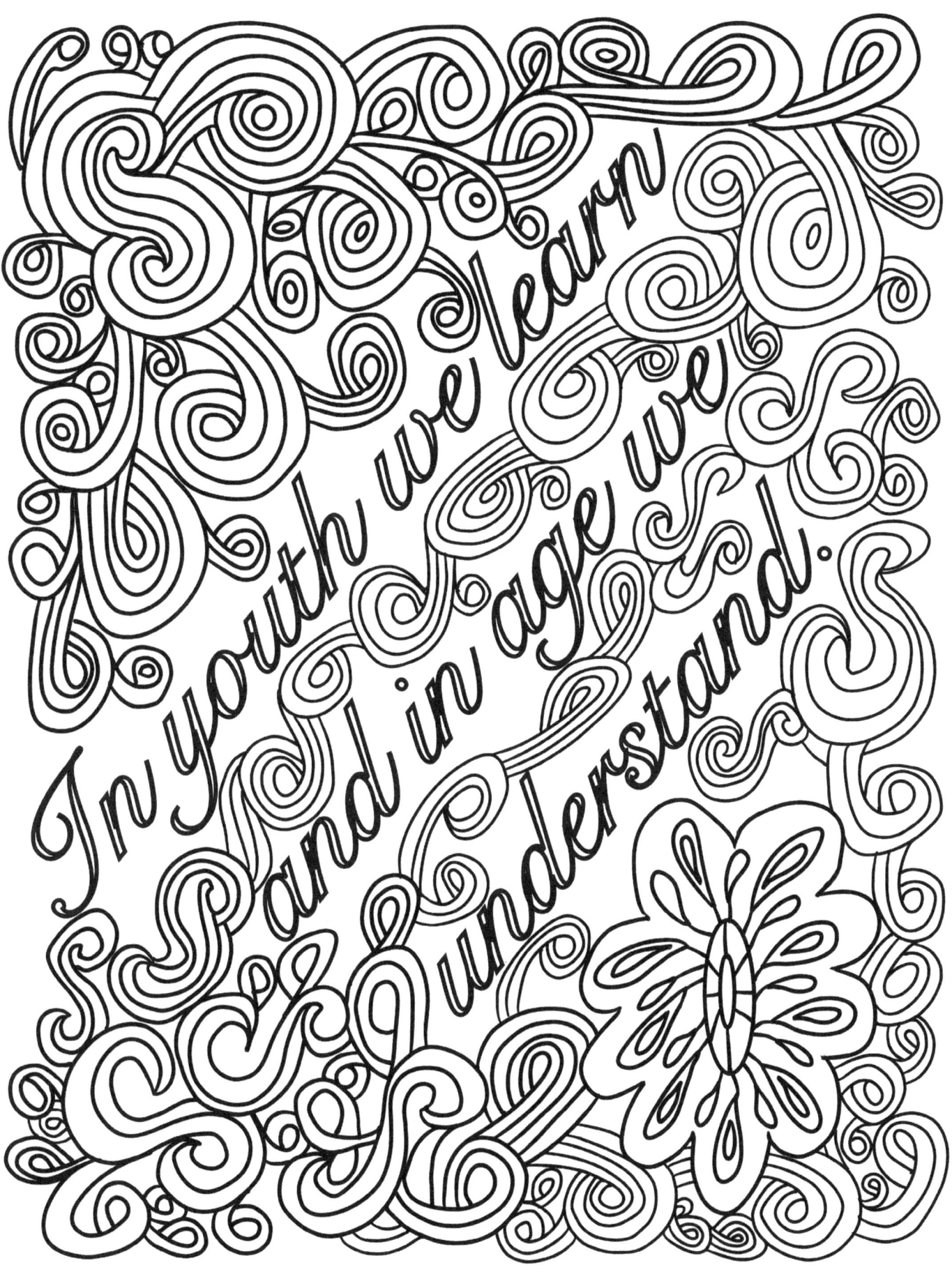

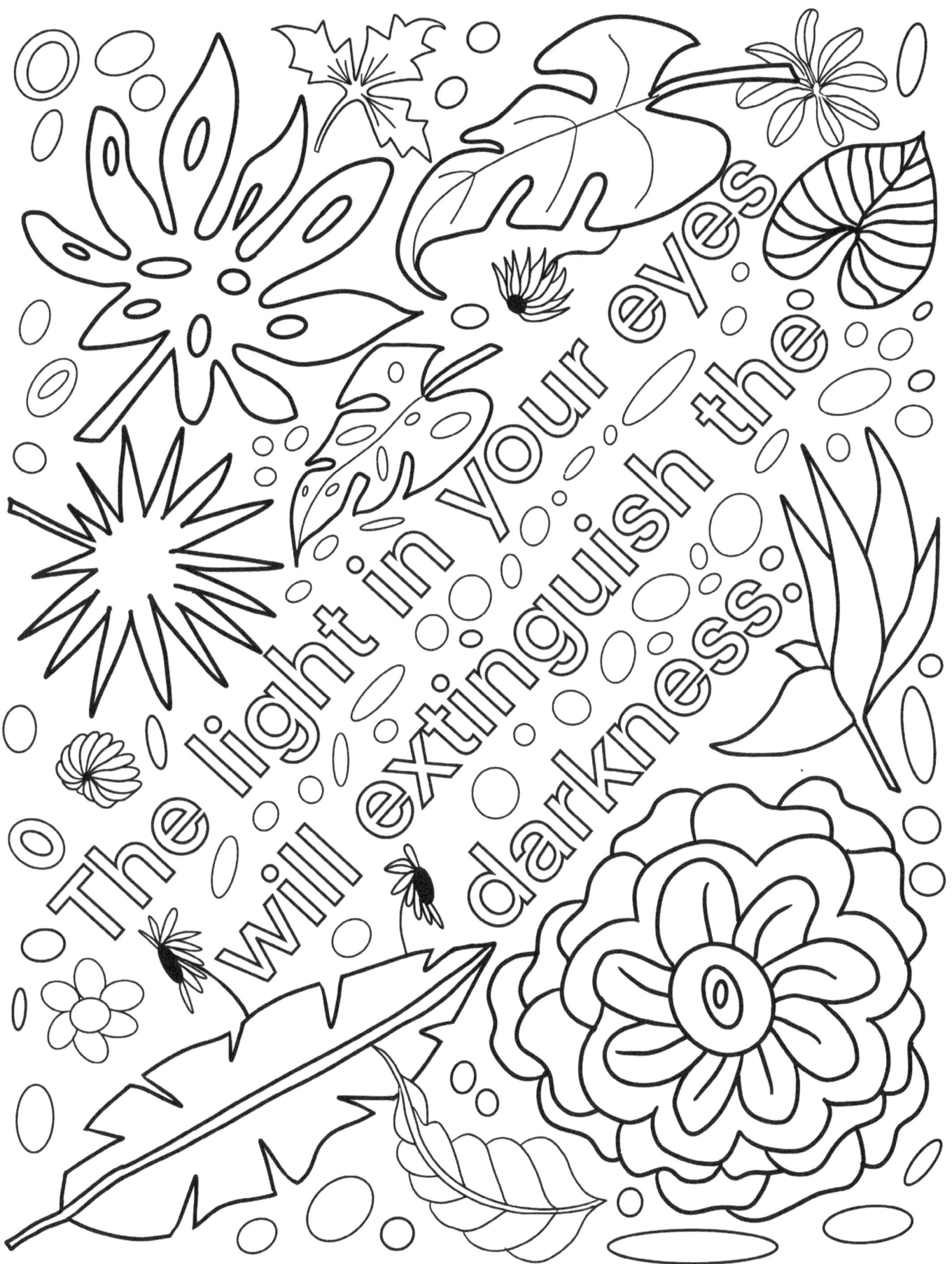

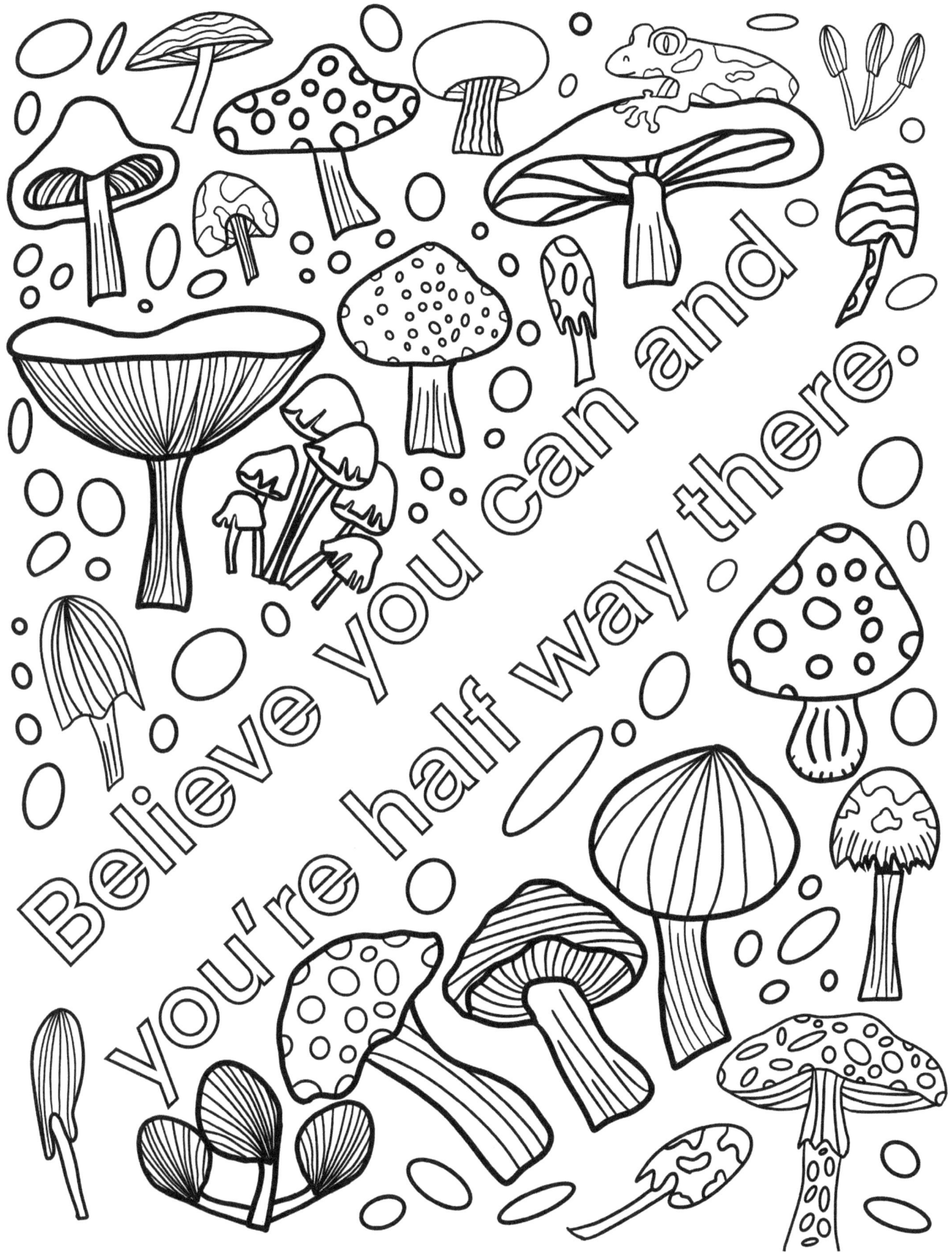

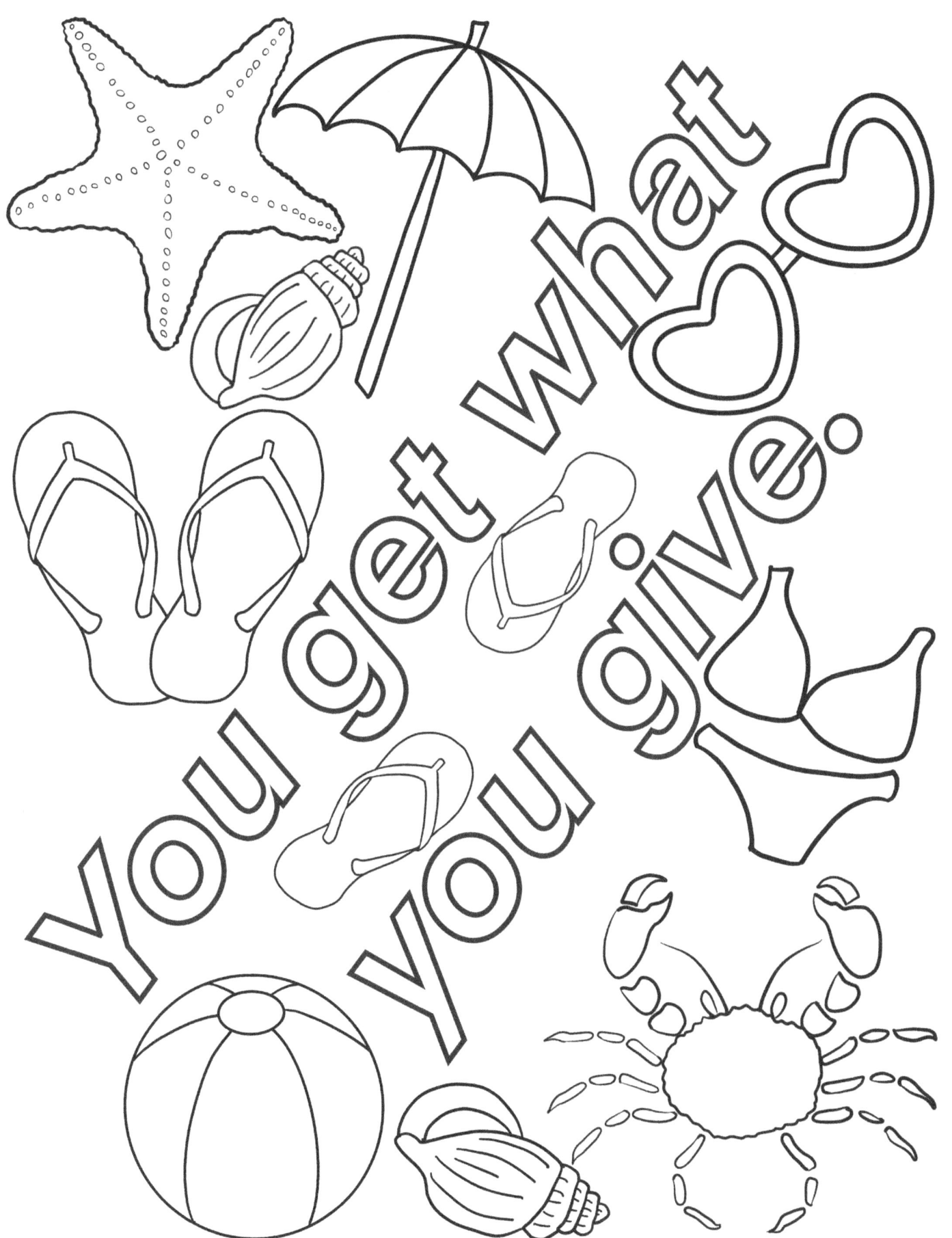

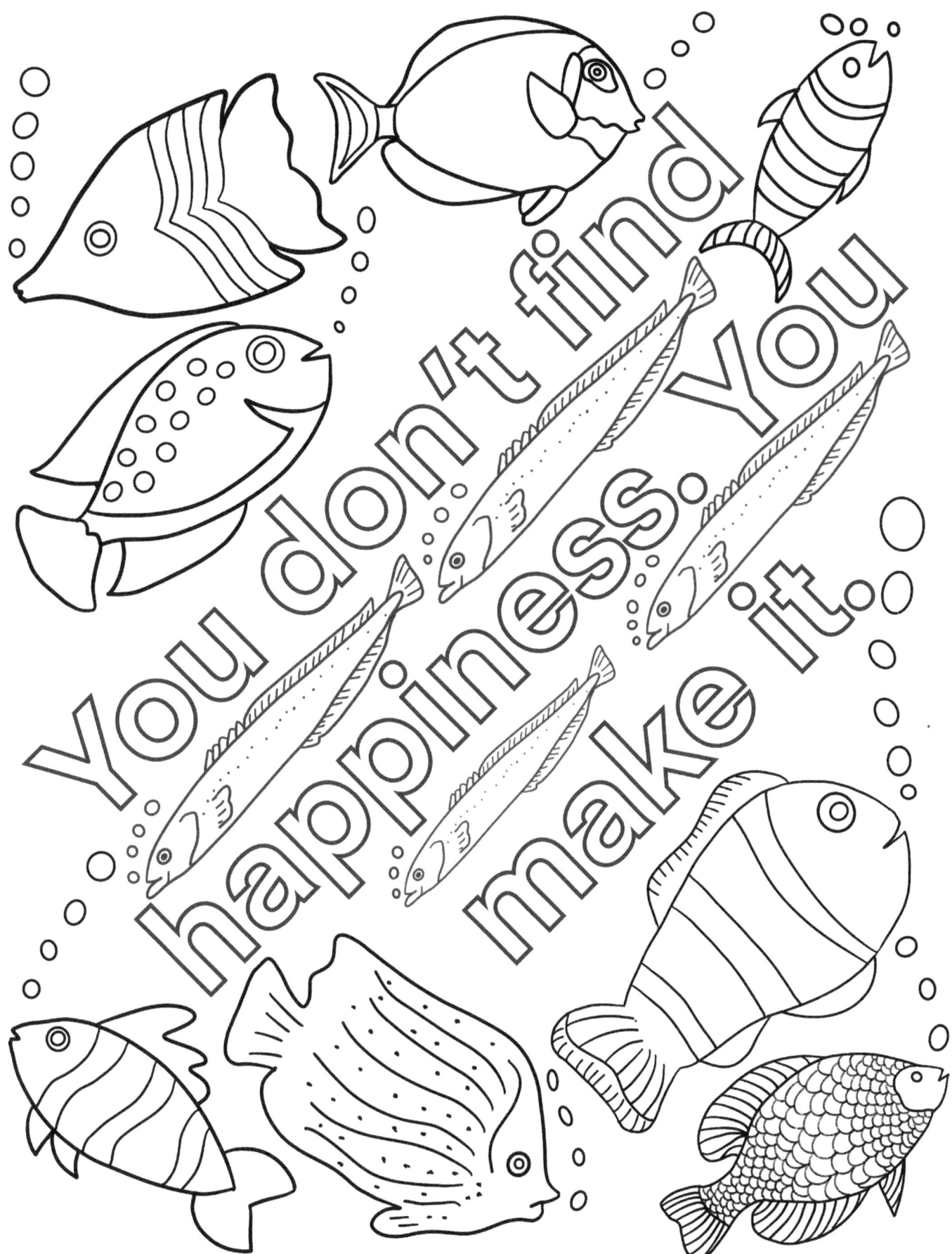

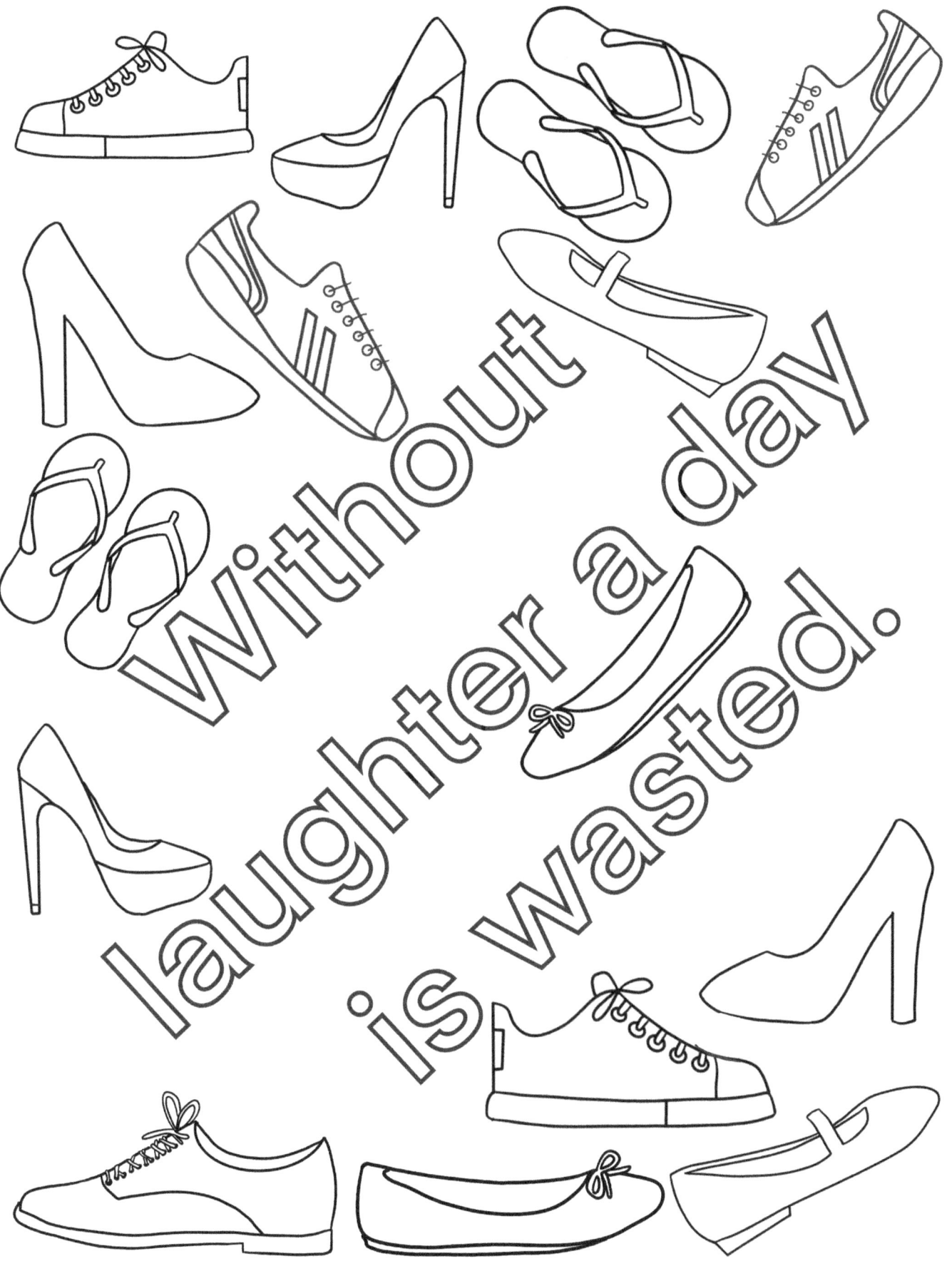

Thanks again for purchasing "Inspiration and Relaxation".

I hope the work you put in to it gave you hours of fun and satisfaction.

I am currently in the process of designing and publishing more adult coloring books for you. Watch for them on Amazon and other bookstore outlets.

Wishing you all the best,

Art King

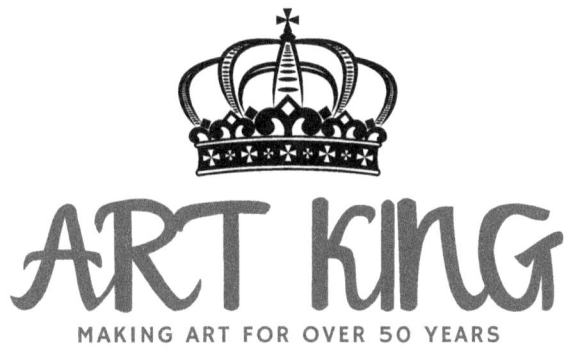